General Introduction to the Old Testament

The Canon

William Henry Green

Baker Book House
Grand Rapids, Michigan

First published in 1898 by
Charles Scribner's Sons
Reprinted 1980 by
Baker Book House Company

ISBN: 0-8010-3755-7

PHOTOLITHOPRINTED BY CUSHING - MALLOY, INC.
ANN ARBOR, MICHIGAN, UNITED STATES OF AMERICA

PREFACE

ANY ONE who addresses himself to the study of the Old Testament will desire first to know something of its character. It comes to us as a collection of books which have been and still are esteemed peculiarly sacred. How did they come to be so regarded? Is it due simply to a veneration for antiquity? Is this a collection of the literature of ancient Israel, which later generations prized as a relic of early ages? Is it a body of Hebrew literature to which sanctity was attributed because of its being written in the sacred tongue? Is it a collection of the books containing the best thoughts of the most enlightened men of the Israelitish nation, embodying their religious faith and their conceptions of human duty? Or is it more than all this? Is it the record of a divine revelation, made through duly authorized and accredited messengers sent of God for this purpose?

The first topic which is considered in this volume is accordingly that of the Canon of the Old Testament, which is here treated not theologically but historically. We meet at the outset two opposing views of the growth of the canon: one contained in the statements of the Old Testament itself, the other in the theories of modern critics, based upon the conception that these books gradually acquired a sacredness which did not at first belong to them, and which did not enter into the purpose for which they were written. This is tested on the one hand by the claims which the various writers make for themselves, and on the other by the regard shown for these books by those to whom they were originally given. The various arguments urged by critics in defence of their position that the canon was not completed nor the collection made until several centuries after the time traditionally fixed and currently believed are considered; and reasons are given to show that it might have been and probably was collected by Ezra and Nehemiah or in their time.

The question then arises as to the books of which the Old Testament properly consists. Can the books of which it was originally composed be certainly identified? And are they the same that are now in the Old Testament as we possess it, and neither more nor less? This is answered by tracing in succession the Old Testament as it was accepted by the Jews, as it was sanctioned by our Lord and the inspired writers of the New Testament, and as it has been received in the Christian Church from the beginning. The Apocrypha though declared to be canonical by the Council of Trent, and accepted as such by the Roman Catholic Church, are excluded from the canon by its history traced in the manner just suggested as well as by the character of their contents, which is incompatible with the idea of their authors being divinely inspired.

PRINCETON, N. J.,
     October 3, 1898.

TABLE OF CONTENTS

VI.

VII.

VIII.

IX.

X.

XI.

XII.

TREATISES CONSULTED ON THE CANON

THESE treatises are arranged in the order of their publication, that their position in the discussion may be seen at a glance.

BISHOP COSIN : A Scholastical History of the Canon, 1672.

J. D. MICHAELIS : Review of Oeder's Freye Untersuchung über einige Bücher des Alten Testaments, in the Orientalische und Exegetische Bibliothek, No. 2, 1772.

J. D. MICHAELIS : Review of Semler's Abhandlung von freyer Untersuchung des Canon, in the same, No. 3, 1772.

J. D. MICHAELIS : Review of Hornemann's Observationes ad illustrationem doctrinæ de Canone Veteris Testamenti ex Philone, in the same, No. 9, 1775.

J. G. EICHHORN : Historische Untersuchung über den Kanon des Alten Testaments, in the Repertorium für Biblische und Morgenländische Litteratur, No. 5, 1779.

J. G. EICHHORN : Review of Corrodi's Versuch einer Beleuchtung der Geschichte des Jüdischen und Christlichen Bibel-Kanons, in the Allgemeine Bibliothek der Biblischen Litteratur, Vol. 4, 1792.

J. G. EICHHORN : Einleitung in das Alte Testament, 3d Ed., 1803; 4th Ed., 1823.

G. L. BAUER : Einleitung in die Schriften des Alten Testaments, 3d Ed., 1806.

L. BERTHOLDT : Einleitung in das Alte und Neue Testament, 1812.

E. W. HENGSTENBERG : Die Authentie des Daniel, 1831.

H. A. C. HÄVERNICK : Einleitung in das Alte Testament, 1836.

J. G. HERBST : Einleitung in das Alte Testament, edited by B. Welte, 1840.

F. C. MOVERS : Loci quidam Historiæ Canonis Veteris Testamenti illustrati, 1842.

MOSES STUART : Critical History and Defence of the Old Testament Canon, 1845.

W. M. L. DE WETTE : Einleitung in das Alte Testament, 6th Ed., 1845 ; 8th Ed. by E. Schrader, 1869.

L. HERZFELD : Geschichte des Volkes Israel, Vol. I., 1847; Vol. III., 1863.

A. McCLELLAND : Canon and Interpretation of the Holy Scriptures, 1850.

A. ALEXANDER : The Canon of the Old and New Testaments, 1851.

P. F. KEERL : Die Apokryphen des Alten Testaments, 1852.

K. F. KEIL : Einleitung in das Alte Testament, 1853 ; 2d Ed. translated into English by G. C. M. Douglas, 1869.

H. EWALD : Ueber das suchen und finden sogenannter Makkabäischer Psalmen, in the Jahrbücher der Biblischen Wissenschaft, 1854.

H. EWALD : Ueber die Heiligkeit der Bibel, in the same, 1855.

B. WELTE : Bemerkungen über die Entstehung des alttest. Canons, in the Theologische Quartalschrift, 1855.

P. DE JONG : Disquisitio de Psalmis Maccabaicis, 1857.

G. F. OEHLER : Kanon des Alten Testaments, in Herzog's Real-Encyklopädie, Vol. VII., 1857.

A. DILLMANN : Ueber die Bildung der Sammlung heiliger Schriften Alten Testaments, in the Jahrbücher für Deutsche Theologie, Vol. III., 1858.

F. BLEEK : Einleitung in das Alte Testament, 1860; 4th Ed. by J. Wellhausen, 1878.

B. F. WESTCOTT : The Canon of Scripture, in Smith's Dictionary of the Bible, 1860.

B. F. WESTCOTT : The Bible in the Church, 1866.

J. FÜRST : Der Kanon des Alten Testaments nach den Ueberlieferungen in Talmud und Midrasch, 1868.

L. DIESTEL : Geschichte des Alten Testamentes in der Christlichen Kirche, 1869.

C. EHRT : Abfassungszeit und Abschluss des Psalters, 1869.

J. DERENBOURG : L'Histoire et la Geographie de la Palestine d'après les Thalmuds et les autres Sources Rabbiniques, 1869.

H. STEINER : Kanon des Alten Testaments, in Schenkel's Bibel-Lexicon, 1871.

I. S. BLOCH : Geschichte der Sammlung der Althebräischen Literatur, 1876.

W. L. ALEXANDER : Canon, in Kitto's Cyclopædia of Biblical Literature, 1876.

H. L. STRACK : Kanon des Alten Testaments, in Herzog-Plitt's Real-Encyklopädie, Vol. VII., 1880.

S. DAVIDSON : The Canon of the Bible, 1880.

W. ROBERTSON SMITH : The Old Testament in the Jewish Church, 1st Ed., 1881 ; 2d Ed., 1892.

G. A. MARX (DALMAN) : Traditio Rabbinorum Veterrima de Librorum Veteris Testamenti Ordine atque Origine, 1884.

F. BUHL : Kanon und Text des Alten Testaments, 1891.

S. R. DRIVER : An Introduction to the Literature of the Old Testament, 1st Ed., 1891 ; 6th Ed., 1897.

H. E. RYLE : The Canon of the Old Testament, 1892.

E. KÖNIG : Einleitung in das Alte Testament, 1893.

G. WILDEBOER : The Origin of the Canon of the Old Testament. Translated by B. W. Bacon, edited by G. F. Moore, 1895.

HISTORY OF INTRODUCTION TO THE OLD TESTAMENT [1]

INTRODUCTION, as a technical term, is of comparatively modern date, and borrowed from the German. It was introduced as a generic designation of those studies, which are commonly regarded as preliminary to the interpretation of the Scriptures. As a science or a branch of systematic learning, Introduction is of modern growth. The early Christian writers were either not sufficiently aware of its importance, or imperfectly provided with the means of satisfactorily treating it. Their attention was directed chiefly to the doctrinal contents of Scripture, and it was only when the genuineness or divine authority of some part or the whole was called in question, that they seem to have considered these preliminary subjects as at all important ; as for instance, when the attack upon the Pentateuch by Celsus, and on Daniel by Porphyry, excited Origen and others to defend them, an effect extending only to the Evidences of Revealed Religion and the Canon of Scripture. The most ancient writings that can be described as general treatises upon this subject are by the two most eminent Fathers of the fourth century, Augustin and Jerome. The four books of the

[1] This brief sketch is extracted from an unpublished lecture of my former friend, preceptor, and colleague, Dr. Joseph Addison Alexander, for many years the ornament and pride of Princeton Theological Seminary. It was written in 1843, and is here inserted as a memento of a brilliant scholar and in humble acknowledgment of indebtedness to his instructions.

former de Doctrina Christiana contain, according to his own description, præcepta tractandarum Scripturarum, and belong therefore chiefly to Hermeneutics. He was ignorant of Hebrew, but his strength of intellect and ingenuity enabled him to furnish many valuable maxims of interpretation. Jerome's book was called "Libellus de optimo interpretandi genere." It is chiefly controversial and of much less value than Augustin's.

The first work which appeared under the name of Introduction was in Greek, the Εἰσαγωγὴ εἰς τὰς Θείας γραφάς of Adrian. Its date is doubtful, and its contents restricted to the style and diction of the sacred writers. An imperfect attempt to methodize the subject was made by Eucherius, Bishop of Lyons, in the fifth century; but the first important advance was made in the sixth century by Cassiodorus, a Benedictine monk, in his work "De Institutione Divinarum Scripturarum," which treats especially the subject of the Canon and of Hermeneutics, and was the standard work in this department through the Middle Ages.

The philological branches of the subject were first treated in detail after the Reformation. The earliest important works of this kind were the "Officina Biblica of Walther" in 1636, and Bishop Walton's "Prolegomena to the London Polyglott" in 1657, which is particularly rich in reference to Biblical Philology and Criticism. The insidious attacks on the divine authority of Scripture by Hobbes and Spinoza, in the latter part of the seventeenth century, called forth as its professed defender Richard Simon, a Romish priest of great ingenuity and considerable learning, but of unsound principles. His Critical Histories of the Old and New Testaments provoked much censure, and gave occasion to the first systematic Introduction to the Old Testament, that of Carpzov, which appeared in 1721, and is chiefly occupied with the evidences of revealed religion and with hermeneutics.

In the eighteenth century, Introduction rose to great importance, and the writers on it exercised great influence. The principles which Simon had obscurely recommended, were avowed and carried out by Semler and his followers, who introduced a general scepticism as to the canonical authority of some books and the inspiration of the whole. The Bible now began to be studied and expounded as a classic, with reference merely to the laws of taste. Upon this principle the great work of Eichhorn was constructed, the first complete Introduction to the books of the Old Testament, the influence of which has been incalculably great in giving an infidel character to modern German exegesis. The counteracting influence of Jahn, a learned Roman Catholic professor at Vienna, has been lessened by his great inferiority to Eichhorn, both in taste and genius, and his equal want of judgment as to some important points. Another valuable work on Introduction from a Roman Catholic source is that of Herbst, Professor in Tübingen, edited after the author's death by his colleague Welte in 1840, and greatly improved by his sound conservative additions. Eichhorn's work, which first appeared in 1780, and in a fourth edition more than forty years after, is in several volumes; but the same general principles of unbelief are taught in a compendious form with great skill and talent by De Wette, one of the most eminent of living German theologians.[1] His Introduction to the Old Testament, filling a moderate octavo, is convenient as presenting a compendious view of the whole subject, with minute and ample references to the best authorities. His views, however, as to in-

---

[1] De Wette died 1849.

spiration are completely infidel. Hengstenberg, Professor at Berlin, a leading writer of the Christian or believing school, began a conservative reaction on the Protestant side by publishing at intervals a series of works upon detached parts of the subject; and one of his pupils, Hävernick of Rostock, with the same principles as Hengstenberg, but less clear and judicious, has just finished a systematic work upon the whole of it.

It may be proper to add that most of the works which have been described or mentioned comprehend only a part of Introduction in its widest sense, the application of the name being different as to extent in different systems. Almost all the systematic works on Introduction exclude Antiquities or Archæology, as so extensive and so unconnected with the others as to be treated more conveniently apart. This is not the case, however, with the only comprehensive work in English on the general subject, that of Horne—a work which cannot be too highly recommended for the soundness of its principles, its Christian spirit, its methodical arrangement, and the vast amount of valuable information which it certainly contains. Its faults are that it is a compilation, and as such contains opinions inconsistent with each other, and in some cases even contradictory, and also that the style is heavy, and the plan too formal and mechanically systematic.

Little need be added to this sketch, written more than fifty years ago. The reaction begun by Hengstenberg, was vigorously continued by Keil and Kurtz, and after them by Noesgen. Bleek and Stähelin, who still belonged to the elder school of critics, were disposed to take a moderate position, and to recede from some of the more advanced conclusions of their predecessors. This tendency was suddenly checked, however, by the rise of the extreme school of Reuss, Wellhausen, and Kuenen, which is now in the ascendant; so that even evangelical scholars, like Strack and König, largely accept their conclusions, and seek to reconcile them with faith ·in the inspiration of the Scriptures. An able and determined revolt against these destructive opinions has of late been initiated by prominent university-bred pastors, such as Adolph Zahn of Stuttgart, Edouard Rupprecht of Bavaria, Hoedemaker of Amsterdam, and Stosch of Berlin, who stand on thoroughly conservative ground.

In Great Britain a tenth edition of Horne's Introduction was prepared by Dr. Samuel Davidson, and largely rewritten by him with a large infusion of German learning and critical ideas, though still maintaining conservative positions. Subsequently he published an Introduction of his own, in which his former conservative conclusions were completely reversed. It was, however, the brilliant and eloquent Robertson Smith, Professor at Aberdeen and then at Cambridge, who was chiefly instrumental in introducing advanced critical opinions among English readers. Dr. Driver's Introduction to the Literature of the Old Testament has contributed still further to spread these views, and give them that measure of popularity to which they have attained. Yet conservative views have not lacked stanch defenders, as in " Isaiah One and his Book One," by Principal Douglas of Glasgow, and "Lex Mosaica," edited by Dr. Valpy French, with nearly a score of able collaborators.

GENERAL INTRODUCTION TO THE OLD TESTAMENT

INTRODUCTION to the Old Testament in the widest sense of the term would include whatever is preliminary or auxiliary to the exegetical study and correct understanding of this portion of the sacred volume. But the subjects which would thus be embraced within it are too numerous and of too heterogeneous a character to be profitably pursued together, or to be classed under a single name. It is accordingly in ordinary usage restricted to a definite range of subjects, viz. : those which concern the literary history and criticism of the Old Testament. Other branches important to the interpreter, such as Biblical Geography, Antiquities, and Natural History, Apologetics, and Hermeneutics can best be treated separately.

Introduction, in the limited and technical sense already explained, is divided into General and Special. General Introduction has to do with those topics which concern the entire volume considered as a whole ; Special Introduction with those which relate to its several parts, or to the individual books of which it consists, such as the questions of date, authorship, integrity or freedom from adulteration, the character of the composition, etc.

General Introduction to the Old Testament, which is the subject of the present volume, is an inquiry into

I. The Collection and Extent of the Canon.

II. The History and Criticism of the Text.

The history of the text must be traced both in respect

to its external form and its internal substance. In studying the former it is necessary to consider

1. The original form of the text, or the Languages in which it was written.

2. The mode of its transmission, viz., by Manuscripts.

3. The additional forms in which it exists, viz., Ancient Versions.

This must be followed by an examination into

4. The internal history of the substance of the text and its present condition.

The way is now prepared for

5. The Criticism of the text, or a consideration of the means available for the detection and correction of any errors which may have crept into it, the proper mode of their application and the result accomplished by them.

THE CANON OF THE OLD TESTAMENT

I

THE CANON

The Old Testament consists of a number of separate books or treatises, which were written by different authors at various periods of time. The questions naturally arise, Why have they all been united thus in one volume? When and how did this take place? Are all that it contains rightfully included in it? Does it contain all the books that properly belong to it?

This collection of books is naturally called the Canon of the Old Testament. This term is derived from the Greek word κανών, which originally denoted "any straight rod," whence it was applied to a rod used in measuring, as a carpenter's rule; and thence metaphorically to any rule whatever, "anything that serves to regulate or determine other things," as the rules or canons of grammar or of rhetoric; and the best Greek writers were by the Alexandrian grammarians called "canons," as being models or standards of literary excellence.[1] It occurs in two passages in the New Testament (Gal. vi. 16; 2 Cor. x. 13–16), in the sense of *rule* or *measure*. In the writings of the Christian Fathers the expressions "the canon of the church," "the canon of the truth," "the canon of the faith," are used to denote the body of

---

[1] Liddell and Scott's Greek Lexicon, s.v.

Christian doctrine as forming the recognized rule of belief. In like manner " the canon of Scripture," or " the canonical Scriptures," became the accepted designation of that body of writings which constitutes the inspired rule of faith and practice.[1] The assertion of Semler, Eichhorn, and others, that " canon " simply means *list* in this connection, and that canonical or canonized books denotes the list of books sanctioned by the Church to be read in public worship, overlooks the primary and proper signification of the term.

[1] The history and usage of this word is very carefully traced by K A. Credner. Zur Geschichte des Kanons, pp. 1–68.

II

TESTIMONY OF THE BIBLE IN REGARD TO THE
FORMATION OF THE CANON

WHILE the Bible does not profess to give a complete
history of the formation of the Canon, it contains important statements concerning it, which must have their
place in any reliable account of the matter; otherwise
all will be left to vague conjecture and arbitrary theorizing. Express provision is said to have been made both
for the careful custody of the first completed portion of
the sacred canon, and for making the people acquainted
with its contents. "And it came to pass, when Moses
had made an end of writing the words of this law in a
book, until they were finished, that Moses commanded
the Levites, who bare the ark of the covenant of Jehovah, saying, Take this book of the law, and put it by the
side of the ark of the covenant of Jehovah your God,
that it may be there for a witness against thee" (Deut.
xxxi. 24–26). It was thus placed in the charge of the
priests to be kept by them along side of the most sacred
vessel of the sanctuary, and in its innermost and holiest
apartment. This was in accordance with the usage of
the principal nations of antiquity. The Romans, Greeks,
Phœnicians, Babylonians, and Egyptians had their
sacred writings, which were jealously preserved in
their temples, and entrusted to the care of officials specially designated for the purpose. Moses also commanded the priests and elders of the people "At the
end of every seven years, in the set time of the year of

11

release, in the feast of tabernacles, when all Israel is come to appear before Jehovah thy God in the place which he shall choose, thou shalt read this law before all Israel in their hearing. Assemble the people, the men and the women and the little ones, and thy stranger that is within thy gates, that they may hear, and that they may learn, and fear Jehovah your God, and observe to do all the words of this law; and that their children, which have not known, may hear, and learn to fear Jehovah your God, as long as ye live in the land whither ye go over Jordan to possess it " (Deut. xxxi. 10–13). And it was still further enjoined that the future king should " write him a copy of this law in a book, out of that which is before the priests the Levites ; and it shall be with him, and he shall read therein all the days of his life ; that he may learn to fear Jehovah his God, to keep all the words of this law and these statutes to do them " (Deut. xvii. 18, 19). And the following direction was given to Joshua, the immediate successor of Moses in the leadership of the people: "This book of the law shall not depart out of thy mouth, but thou shalt meditate therein day and night, that thou mayest observe to do according to all that is written therein " (Josh. i. 8).

According to the uniform testimony of all the sacred historians, the law of Moses, thus carefully guarded and made obligatory upon the people and their rulers, was ever after regarded as canonical and divinely authoritative, and that even in the most degenerate times. The punctilious obedience rendered to it by Joshua is repeatedly noticed in the course of his life (*e.g.*, Josh. xi. 15). Canaanites were left in the land to prove Israel " whether they would hearken unto the commandments of Jehovah, which he commanded their fathers by the hand of Moses " (Judg. iii. 4). Saul forfeited his kingdom by failing to comply with a requirement of the law,

which Samuel had charged him to execute (1 Sam. xv.).
David charged Solomon to obey the law of Moses (1
Kin. ii. 3).   David is repeatedly commended for keeping the law (1 Kin. iii. 14, ix. 4, xi. 34, 38).   Solomon's
compliance with the law of Moses in the worship instituted in the temple is noted (2 Chron. viii. 13); and he
impressed upon the people their obligation to obey it
(1 Kin. viii. 56–58, 61).   The prophet Ahijah denounced
Jeroboam for his disobedience to the commandments of
Jehovah (1 Kin. xiv. 7–16).   King Asa commanded the
people to keep the law (2 Chron. xiv. 4).   Jehoshaphat
sent a deputation throughout all the cities of Judah to
teach the people the book of the law (2 Chron. xvii. 9).
The law of Moses was observed under Joash (2 Chron.
xxiii. 18, xxiv. 6).   Amaziah is said to have acted in accordance with the law of Moses (2 Kin. xiv. 6; 2 Chron.
xxv. 4).   Hezekiah kept the commandments which Jehovah commanded Moses (2 Kin. xviii. 6; 2 Chron. xxx.
16).   Manasseh's gross transgressions of the law of
Moses were denounced by the prophets (2 Kin. xxi. 2–
16).   Josiah bound the people in solemn covenant to
obey the law of Moses (2 Kin. xxiii. 3, 24, 25; 2 Chron.
xxxiv. 14, 30–32).   The exile of both Israel and Judah
is attributed to their infractions of the law of Moses (2
Kin. xvii. 7–23, xviii. 12; 2 Chron. xxxiii. 8; Dan. ix. 11,
13; Neh. i. 7–9, ix. 14–30).   The first colony of returned
exiles recognized the authority of the law of Moses
(Ezra iii. 2, vi. 16–18).   The book of the law was read
and expounded to the people by Ezra and the Levites
(Neh. viii. 1–8), and all solemnly pledged themselves to
obey it (Neh. x. 28, 29, xiii. 1–3).

We read of an addition being made to the book of
the law in Josh. xxiv. 26 : " And Joshua wrote these
words in the book of the law of God." The reference
is to the covenant transaction at Shechem, in which

the people are reminded of what Jehovah had done for their fathers and for themselves, and they in turn pledged to him their faithful service. It was an appropriate appendix to the law, recording God's gracious leadings and the fulfilment of his promises, and the engagement of the people to obey his requirements. It would thus, like the law itself, be a witness against the people in all time to come, if they forsook the LORD.

No mention is made of any subsequent addition to the book of the law, but a fact is stated in 1 Sam. x. 25, which is of some consequence in this connection. It is there said that upon the selection of Saul to be king, "Samuel told the people the manner of the kingdom," *i.e.*, he expounded to them the regulations belonging to this new form of government, the rights and duties of both the king and his subjects, "and wrote it in a book and laid it up before Jehovah." This important paper relating to the constitution of the monarchy in Israel was deposited for safe-keeping in the sacred tabernacle. It is an act analogous to that of Moses in making a similar disposition of the fundamental constitution of Israel as the people of God, and so far confirmatory of it. It has sometimes been inferred that what was thus done with a paper of national importance, must *a fortiori* have been also done with each fresh addition to the volume of God's revelation; and as a complete canon of Scripture was preserved in the second temple,[1] so the pre-exilic sanctuary must have contained a standard copy, not merely of the law of Moses, but of the whole word of God, as far as it was written. There is, however, no historical confirmation of this conjecture.

[1] Josephus, Ant., iii. 1, 7, v. 1, 17 ; Jewish War, vii. 5, 5 ; Life of Josephus, § 75.

When the temple of Solomon was built, the copy of the law previously kept in the tabernacle was without doubt transferred to it. The direction which placed it in the custody of the priests was still in force, and the change of the sanctuary made no alteration in the sacredness of what had before been deposited in it. This is not disproved, as has been alleged,[1] by 1 Kin. viii. 9 and the parallel passage 2 Chron. v. 10, where it is declared that "there was nothing in the ark" when it was removed to the temple " save the two tables of stone, which Moses put there at Horeb." The book of the law was put (מִצַּד) " by the side of the ark," not within it. Whether it was still put by the side of the ark, after this was deposited in the temple and was no longer liable to be transported from place to place, cannot be certainly known. But that it was kept somewhere in the temple appears from the express mention of it in 2 Kin. xxii. 8. It is there stated that the book of the law, explicitly identified with the law of Moses (xxiii. 24, 25), which had been neglected and lost sight of during the ungodly reigns of Manasseh and Amon, was found again in the temple in the reign of Josiah. This was but a short time before the destruction of the city and temple by Nebuchadnezzar and the Babylonish captivity.

In all probability the book of the law belonging to the temple perished when the temple was burned (2 Kin. xxv. 9), but this did not involve the destruction of the law itself, numerous copies of which must have been in existence. Every king was required to have one for his own use (Deut. xvii. 18). The kings of Judah, who are commended for observing the law, must have possessed it. And it is explicitly stated that in the coronation of king Joash Jehoiada, the high priest,

---

[1] De Wette's Einleitung (6th edition), § 14, note *f*.

gave him "the crown and the testimony." The testimony can only mean here as elsewhere the law as an authoritative declaration of the will of God (Ps. xix. 7, lxxviii. 5 ; 1 Kin. ii. 3 ; 2 Kin. xxiii. 3). The transaction described was the formal presentation to a monarch, upon his accession to the throne, of a copy of the law to be the guide of his reign. The judges appointed by Jehoshaphat were to decide questions arising under the law (2 Chron. xix. 10), and must have been able to make themselves familiar with its contents. The commission sent by him to visit the cities of Judah took a copy of the law with them (2 Chron. xvii. 8, 9). Solomon's urgent admonition to the people to walk in the statutes of Jehovah and to keep his commandments assumes their knowledge of what they were expected to obey (1 Kin. viii. 61). The numerous allusions to the law in all the subsequent books of the old Testament [1] indicate familiarity with it on the part of the sacred writers. Ps. i. 4 [2] describes the pious by saying "his delight is in the law of Jehovah, and in his law he doth meditate day and night." The admiration and affection for the law expressed in such passages as Ps. xix. 7–11, xl. 7, 8,[3] and the exhortations and rebukes of the prophets based upon the requirements of the law imply an acquaintance with it such as could only be produced by its diffusion among the people. In the persecution of Antiochus Epiphanes various persons were found to be in possession of the sacred books ;[4] the same was doubtless the case in the period now under review. The returning exiles governed themselves by the direc-

[1] See my Higher Criticism of the Pentateuch, pp. 52–58.

[2] This Psalm is certainly older than Jeremiah, who makes use of ver. 3 in xvii. 8.

[3] These Psalms are ascribed to David in their titles, the correctness of which there is no good reason for discrediting.

[4] 1 Macc. i. 56, 57. Josephus, Ant., xii. 5, 4.

tions of the law of Moses (Ezra iii. 2, vi. 18); and Ezra came up from captivity with the law of God in his hand (vii. 14), facts which sufficiently prove that the law had neither perished nor lost its authority.

But the law of Moses was not the only book that was invested with divine authority. It will be sufficient here to note the fact that the prophets were acknowledged messengers of Jehovah, who spoke in his name and at his bidding. What they uttered was the word of Jehovah and the law of God (Isa. i. 10). The calamities which befel Israel and Judah are attributed to their disobeying the law, both that which was commanded their fathers and that which was sent to them by the prophets (2 Kin. xvii. 13; Neh. ix. 29, 30; Dan. ix. 5, 6; Zech. vii. 12). The word of Jehovah by the prophets had, of course, the same binding authority when written as when orally delivered. Reference is made (Isa. xxxiv. 16) to "the book of Jehovah," in which the antecedent prophecy could be found and its exact fulfilment noted. Daniel ix. 2 speaks of "the books" in which a prophecy of Jeremiah, then on the eve of fulfilment, was contained. The books of the prophets from the time that they were first written formed a component part of the revealed will of God, and belonged of necessity to the canonical Scriptures.

To this extent, then, the statements of the Bible are explicit in regard to the formation of the canon. The law written by Moses was by his direction deposited in the sanctuary as the divinely obligatory standard of duty for Israel. To this was added by Joshua a solemn engagement on the part of the people to obey it. Though this law was grossly transgressed at times by the people and their rulers, its supreme authority found repeated and emphatic recognition, and was attended by divine sanctions culminating in the overthrow of both the kingdoms of Israel and Judah. The book of the law, which was kept in the temple, probably perished when the latter was burned. But other copies escaped, and the law was still in the hands of the people at the close of the exile. No intimation is given that the books of the prophets were as yet united with the law in the same volume, but they are classed with it as emanating from the same divine source, being equally the word and law of God, with a like claim to unfaltering obedience.

III

THE CRITICAL THEORY OF THE FORMATION OF THE CANON

EICHHORN,[1] who has been called the Father of Higher Criticism, did not hesitate to admit that the laws of Moses were deposited by his direction in the sanctuary by the side of the ark, as a divinely given and authoritative code agreeably to the statement in Deut. xxxi. 25, 26. But as the Pentateuch was more and more discredited, and belief in its Mosaic authorship was abandoned, later critics changed their attitude accordingly. The present critical position in this matter is well represented by Dillmann,[2] and may be briefly stated as follows : If Moses had written the Pentateuch or any book of laws it would, as a matter of course, have been thenceforward, in the proper and fullest sense of the word, canonical. His work, however, was not writing, but acting, establishing institutions, and enkindling a new spiritual life. After his death, attempts were made, from time to time, to reduce his statutes and ordinances to writing for public or private use without producing a body of laws universally accepted as authoritative, for these collections were liable to be superseded by others more complete or more perspicuous. The book of the law found in the temple in the reign of Josiah (2 Kin. xxii. 8) was the culmination of all attempts in this direction, embodying both what was gained from the

---

[1] Einleitung, 4th edition, p. 20.
[2] Jahrbücher für Deutsche Theologie, III., p. 432 ff.

experience of the past and the instructions of the prophets with special adaptation to the needs of the present. This was at once accepted by both king and people, who solemnly bound themselves to obey its requirements. This book was Deuteronomy,[1] and was the first written law having canonical authority. During the exile the Pentateuch was completed in its present form by the addition of the priestly laws and other constituents. This was brought to Jerusalem by Ezra when he came up from the captivity, and, as is related in Neh. viii.–x., was read before the assembled people, who thereupon pledged themselves to observe all that it commanded. By this transaction the Pentateuch, which was thenceforth denominated the law, or the law of Moses, was made canonical, and was ever after accepted as supremely authoritative. This is not only the first division of the canon, but the critics insist that it constituted the first canon, and that it is all that was regarded as canonical and authoritative in the time of Ezra. He was a scribe of the law (Ezra vii. 6, 12, 21); he prepared his heart to seek the law and do it and teach it to Israel (ver. 10); he went to Jerusalem with the law of God in his hand (ver. 14); he bound the people by a written engagement (Neh. ix. 38) and a solemn oath (x. 29) to obey the law in every particular. This alone, it is urged, constituted at that time the publicly sanctioned and authoritative divine canon.

The books of the prophets, which stand next in the

[1] In 1858, when the article was written from which the preceding statement has been condensed, Dillmann still held what was at that time the common critical opinion, that the book of the law found in the temple was the entire Pentateuch, which had recently been completed by the addition of Deuteronomy. The critical revolution introduced by Graf and Wellhausen led to a sudden reversal of opinions in this respect, and it is now claimed that the completion of the Pentateuch was the work of priests in or after the Babylonish exile.

order of the Hebrew Bible, are, in the opinion of the critics, not only a second division of the canon, but, historically speaking, were a second canon additional to the first, and incorporated with it at a later time. These books, it is said, were privately circulated at first, and were highly esteemed by the pious who possessed them. But they had no public official authority until they were formally united with the canon. This second collection included what are called the former and the latter prophets. The former prophets are the four historical books according to the original enumeration, Joshua, Judges, Samuel, and Kings, which trace the history of the chosen people and of God's dealings with them in a direct line from the death of Moses to the Babylonish captivity. These follow immediately after the Pentateuch, as they continue the history from the point at which it closes. They are called the former prophets because in the order of the canon they precede the strictly prophetical books, which are accordingly termed the latter prophets. Of these there are likewise four in the original enumeration, viz.: three major prophets, so named because of their superior size, Isaiah, Jeremiah, and Ezekiel, and twelve minor prophets, whose writings, on account of their inferior size, are classed together as one book. A considerable time after the formation of the first canon by Ezra this second canon of the books of the prophets was added to it, so that the canon, as thus constituted, consisted of the law and the prophets ; and for a length of time these are all that were reckoned canonical.

At a still later period, however, a third canon was formed of other books which were thought worthy of being associated with the preceding collections. As these were of a somewhat miscellaneous character and incapable of being included under any more descriptive

designation, they were simply called by the general
name K'thubhim [1] (כְּתוּבִים) *writings*, or by the Greek
equivalent, Hagiographa (ἁγιόγραφα), *sacred writings.*
These include the three large poetical books, Psalms
(תְהִלִּים), Proverbs (מִשְׁלֵי), and Job (אִיּוֹב), from whose
initials have been formed the memorial word אֱמֶת
truth; then the five small books called Megilloth, *rolls,*
because they were written on separate rolls for synagogue use, viz.: the Song of Solomon, Ruth, Lamentations, Ecclesiastes, Esther, and, finally, the three books,
as originally numbered, Daniel, Ezra (including Nehemiah), and Chronicles. Thus, by successive steps in
the course of time, the canon reached its final form, embracing the Law, the Prophets, and the K'thubhim,[2] or
Hagiographa.

The critics acknowledge that there is no historical
testimony to the existence of the successive stages,
which they profess to find, in the formation of the
canon.[3] All the testimony in the case is, in fact, directly

---

[1] Pronounced kᵉthūvīm.

[2] Bertholdt, Einleitung, p. 81, gives to this term the purely fanciful
definition, " books lately inserted in the canon," on the false assumption that the root כָּתַב, *to write,* has the sense "to inscribe in the
canon." K'thubhim, as the technical name of the third division of the
canon, is not to be derived, as some have claimed, from כָּתוּב, *it is
written,* the common formula of citation from the Scriptures, nor
from כָּתַב in the sense of *Scripture,* as indicating that it is a part of
the sacred volume. It is properly the passive participle of כָּתַב, *to
write,* used as a noun, and meaning " Writings," not in a depreciating
sense, as Dillmann alleges (Jahrb. f. D. Theol., III., p. 430), " in contrast with the law and the prophets they were nothing but ' writings,'
to which no such distinguishing quality as Mosaic or prophetic belongs." Their association with the law and the prophets in the canon
sufficiently shows that they were equally regarded as the inspired word
and vested with divine authority. They are "writings" by way of
eminence, ranking above mere ordinary human productions. Com-
pare the Greek γραφαί and the English " Bible."

[3] Wildeboer, The Origin of the Canon, p. 114 : " We have not at

opposed to it. It is claimed, however, that there are other proofs sufficient to establish it.

1. It is alleged that there are several books in the canon which were not yet in existence when the law was made canonical by Ezra, nor at any time during his life. Ezra, Chronicles, and Ecclesiastes are referred by critics to a time shortly before or after the downfall of the Persian Empire, Esther to that of the Greek domination, and Daniel and several of the Psalms to the period of the Maccabees, nearly three centuries after the canonization of the law.

2. It is argued that the three-fold division of the canon of itself affords a clue to the mode of its formation; it is of such a nature that it can only represent three successive stages in the work of collection. There is no consistent principle of classification such as we would naturally expect to find if the canon had been arranged at any one time by any man or body of men. There are books in the third division which are homogeneous with those in the second, and which, if properly classed, would have been put in the second division. And the only explanation of their standing where they do is that the second division was already closed when these books were added, so that there was no resource but to put them in the third and last division, which must, accordingly, have been formed after the second division was complete. Thus, while the principal books containing the post-Mosaic history of the chosen people are in the second division of the canon, viz.: Joshua, Judges, Samuel, and Kings, there are

our command for the history of the canonization of the second division of the Old Testament books, any such historical testimony as we have for those of the law." Page 136 : " Direct historical statements about the third collection of the Old Testament Scriptures are wanting, as in the case of the second."

other books continuing this same history and of like character in the third division, such as Ezra and Nehemiah, and particularly Chronicles, which is parallel to the history in Samuel and Kings, covering, to a considerable extent, the same period, extracted in part from the same sources, and in numerous sections or paragraphs identical in language. Further, the book of Daniel, instead of standing in the second division with the rest of the books of the prophets, is put in the third division along with books of quite a different description. It is claimed that the only satisfactory solution of these facts is that these books only found admission to the canon after the second division, with which they had affinity, was already regarded as complete and incapable of being reopened. They were, accordingly, put at the end of the third, which was the only division then remaining open.

3. The Samaritans recognize the canonicity of the Pentateuch, but of no other part of the Old Testament. From this it is inferred that their reception of the Pentateuch dates from a time when the law of Moses was all that was canonical with the Jews; and that the subsequent hostility between them and the Samaritans has prevented the latter from accepting the additions afterward made to the canon.

4. The synagogue lessons were, in the first instance, taken exclusively from the law; afterward, lessons from the prophets were read in conjunction with it. The K'thubhim are used only on special occasions, and not in the regular sabbath reading of the Scriptures. This is best explained by assuming that the law alone was canonical at first, that the prophets were next added, and the K'thubhim last of all.

5. The term law is sometimes used, both in Jewish writings and in the New Testament in a comprehensive

sense, embracing the entire Old Testament. At other times the law and the prophets are spoken of either as the principal parts of the Old Testament or as comprehending the whole. This is again regarded as a reminiscence of the time when first the law, and afterward the law and the prophets, constituted the entire canon, so that it became natural to use these names to signify the whole revealed word of God.

6. There are said to be indications in the order of the books in both the second and third divisions of the canon that these were formed gradually in the course of time and not by a single act.

7. The canonicity of certain books, particularly the Song of Solomon, Ecclesiastes, and Esther, was long disputed among the Jews, and the question was not finally decided in their favor until the council at Jamnia, about A.D. 90, or, as some have maintained, even later. The canon, in its present form and compass, could not, it is said, have been definitely fixed until then.

IV

THE DETERMINING PRINCIPLE IN THE FORMATION OF THE CANON

THE critical theory of the formation of the canon rests upon a false notion regarding the real character of the canon and the determining principle in its collection. The fundamental error which underlies all the arguments of the critics on this subject, and vitiates their conclusion, is the assumption that the books of the Old Testament were not written with the design of being held sacred and divinely authoritative; but in the course of time they came to be treated with a veneration, which was not at first accorded to them. This is explicitly avowed by Ewald:[1] "It lies in the original nature of all sacred writings that they become sacred without intending it, and without in human fashion being planned to become so. . . . When the first active life ceases, and men have to look back upon it as the model, conform their lives to its regulations and prescriptions, repeat its songs, and carefully consider its whole history, then they look about eagerly for the best writings which can be serviceable in this respect; and for the most part these have already imperceptibly by their own merit separated themselves from the less suitable, have already been gathered piecemeal, and it only requires some superior oversight to combine them in an enduring manner, and consecrate them more definitely for their present purpose. In respect to a few of the

[1] Jahrbücher der Biblischen Wissenschaft, VII., pp. 77, 78.

less necessary there may for a time be uncertainty and strife; but the need of the time and their own intrinsic value will long since have decided in respect to the principal books. And so what was not itself intended to be sacred, nevertheless becomes sacred as the vehicle of sacred truths and spiritual forces."

To the same purport Dillmann: [1] "For a certain class of theologians the several books of the Old Testament were from the first written with the view of being revered and used by the church and handed down to future generations as sacred; the canon was being formed and enlarged by each new book that was added in the course of centuries; so soon as the last book of this sort had appeared, the canon was completed, and it was now only necessary to collect these books which had appeared one after another, combine them into one whole, and bring them into the fine order in which they now lie before us. This office was performed by some public person or authority qualified for the same by a special divine illumination. This conception of the course of the matter is, to be sure, very simple, and inferred with great logical exactness from certain preconceived dogmatical ideas, but it is unhistorical and therefore untrue. How the canon was formed can only be ascertained in a historical way. And history knows nothing of the individual books having been designed to be sacred from their origin; it also knows nothing of an authority by which, or of a point of time at which, all the writings of the Old Testament were at once united and published as a collection of sacred writings forever closed. On the contrary, all that has hitherto been ascertained and laboriously enough investigated respecting the origin of the books and the transmission of their text forbids us to believe that these writings were from

[1] Jahrb. D. Theol., III., p. 420.

the first regarded sacred and inviolable, as they were in
the opinion of later generations. A historical survey
of these relations shows that these books bore indeed in
themselves from the first those characteristics, on account of which they were subsequently admitted into
the sacred collection, but yet always had first to pass
through a shorter or longer period of verification, and
make trial of the divine power resident within them
upon the hearts of the church before they were out-
wardly and formally acknowledged by it as divine
books."

If now in the opinion of the critics the books of the
Old Testament were written with no intention of their
being held sacred, and they were not in actual fact so
regarded at first, what is the source of the sacredness
which was afterward attached to them? How did they
come to be regarded with that veneration which distinguished them from all other books, and led to their
being formed into a sacred canon? In other words,
what was the guiding principle in the formation of the
canon? To this question different answers have been
given.

Some have held with Eichhorn [1] that the canon was
simply a collection of the early national literature. All
books written before a certain date were highly prized
because of their antiquity, and regarded with a veneration which was not felt for more recent productions.
And as the gathering up of ancient writings would be a

[1] Einleitung, § 5: "Soon after the end of the Babylonish exile
. . . and in order to give to the newly built second temple all the
advantages of the first, a library of its own was founded in it of the
remains of Hebrew literature, which we commonly call the Old Testament." Allgem. Bibliothek d. bibl. Litteratur, IV., p. 254: "Evidently everything was collected, which they possessed from the times
before Artaxerxes, or which it was believed must be referred to so
high an antiquity."

slow and laborious process, and a prolonged search would be necessary and considerable time must elapse before it could be certified that the collection was complete, and no more books remained to be discovered, it is contended that the canon could not have been gathered at once, but must have been the work of time. All this is, however, palpably at variance with the fact that the books of Chronicles make mention of several writings then extant, to which readers are referred for further information, and which must, therefore, have been of earlier date than Chronicles; yet this latter was admitted to the canon, while the former were not.

Others have maintained with Hitzig [1] that the determining feature was the language in which the books were written. Those in the sacred Hebrew tongue were accounted sacred, those in Greek were not. But this is disproved by the same argument as the preceding. The books referred to in Chronicles as historical authorities were of course in Hebrew, yet were not admitted to the canon. And some of the apocryphal books, which never had a place in the canon, were written in Hebrew. This was the case with Ecclesiasticus, the prologue to which speaks of its having been translated out of Hebrew into Greek, and so far from the Hebrew original having been lost at the time of the collection of the canon, a fragment of it is still in existence. Tobit also and 1 Maccabees, according to Jerome, were written in Hebrew, and

---

[1] Die Psalmen, 1836, II., p. 118: " All Hebrew books originating in the time before Christ are canonical, all canonical books are Hebrew, while all written in Greek are reckoned as belonging to the apocrypha. . . . Greek books were excluded from the collection of national writings ; no matter whether they had never existed in a Hebrew original, or this was no longer extant." Thus he insists that the Hebrew originals of Ecclesiasticus and Baruch had already been lost when the canon was collected, and they were then only extant in a Greek translation.

he says that he had seen the Hebrew originals. As Dillmann[1] truly says, "Wherever and however the alleged point of time may be fixed from the days of Ezra down to those of Josephus, we always find, besides those which became canonical, other books written in the sacred tongue still extant, which did not come into the canon, and which were not then lost, but subsequently came to be lost after the final and complete close of the canon, and for the reason that they had not been admitted to it."

But their religious character is so prominent a feature of these writings, and enters so essentially into the exalted position assigned to them and the profound veneration which has been felt for them, that the great majority of critics have confessed that this must be taken into the account in estimating the Old Testament; and that it can neither be regarded as a mere collection of ancient literature nor of writings in the sacred Hebrew tongue. The measure of influence assigned to this pervading characteristic of the sacred writings varies with the spirit of the individual critic all the way from the shallow suggestion of Corrodi[2] that they con-

[1] Ubi supra, p. 422.

[2] The author of the Versuch einer Beleuchtung der Geschichte des Jüdischen und Christlichen Bibelkanons, published anonymously in 1792. G. L. Bauer, Einleitung, 3d edition, page 33, claims that there is no real difference in the various conceptions of the canon. "The common opinion is: All the religious writings inspired of God. Eichhorn says: All the fragments of Hebrew literature. Corrodi: Only such writings as concerned national religion or history, and the criterion of divinity and inspiration was introduced later from the time of Sirach onward. In our opinion, all these views may be united. All the fragments of the ancient Hebrew literature were collected, for almost all had a religious form or concerned sacred history. And that these books were written by inspiration of the Holy Spirit the old world, according to their notions, had little doubt, since they even allowed that a goldsmith and embroiderer was filled with the Spirit

cern the national religion to the far more reverent attitude of Ewald and Dillmann in the extracts before quoted, who appeal to their normative character as presenting the loftiest models and setting forth in their purity the requirements of the religion of Israel, and their spiritual power to nurture and elevate the religious life; to which Robertson Smith [1] adds that all the books of the canon were in full accord with the law of Moses. But even when this view is presented in its highest and best form, it is seriously defective, and completely inverts the order of cause and effect. It is true, as the apostle declares (2 Tim. iii. 16), that every Scripture is profitable for teaching, for reproof, for correction, for instruction which is in righteousness, that the man of God may be complete, furnished completely unto every good work; but it is because it is inspired of God. It is not the religious profit derived from these books which led to their admission into the canon, but it is their being inspired of God to guide the faith and practice of the church—in other words, their canonicity—which makes them profitable to the religious life. They were included in the canon because they were written by men inspired of God for this very purpose.

In order to ascertain the true import of the canoniza-

of God." To the same purport De Wette, Einleitung, 6th edition, section 16: "The two assumptions that the Old Testament was intended to constitute a collection of national writings and that it was a collection of sacred writings, are really one in view of the contents of most of the Old Testament books and the theocratic spirit of Jewish antiquity; for the truly national was also religious. In either case the authors were regarded as inspired, and their writings as the fruit of sacred inspiration."

[1] The Old Testament in the Jewish Church, 2d edition, page 181: "The ultimate criterion by which every book was subjected lay in the supreme standard of the law. Nothing was holy which did not agree with the teaching of the Pentateuch."

tion of the Old Testament, we must examine (1) the claims which its several books make for themselves, and (2) the esteem in which they were held by the people. In Ex. xx. 2, 3, Jehovah announces himself to Israel as their God, who brought them out of the land of Egypt, and bids them have no other god besides himself. And the people solemnly engage to obey all his commands (xix. 8), and enter into formal covenant with him as his people (xxiv. 7, 8).　At every subsequent period of their history the people are reminded of their obligation to Jehovah for delivering them from the bondage of Egypt, and their engagement to be his people and to serve him as their God (Josh. xxiv. 16–18; Judg. vi. 8–10; 1 Sam. xii. 6, 7; 2 Sam. vii. 23, 24; Hos. xii. 9, xiii. 4; Am. ii. 10, iii. 2).　Nothing is plainer on the very surface of the Old Testament from first to last than the recognized fact that Jehovah was the God of Israel and that Israel was his people.　Now the law of Moses claims in all its parts to be the law of Jehovah given through Moses.　The entire legislation of the Pentateuch asserts this for itself in the most positive way and in the most unambiguous terms.　The prophets throughout claim to speak in the name of Jehovah and by his authority, and to declare his will.　What they utter is affirmed to be the word of Jehovah; their standing formula is, Thus saith Jehovah.　To yield to their requirements is to obey Jehovah; to refuse submission to them is to offend against Jehovah.　Jehovah is further the recognized king of Israel.　He guides their history, rewards their obedience, punishes their transgression. The historical books reveal his hand in every turn of their affairs; they authoritatively declare his will and purposes, as they are manifested in his providential dealings with them.　The law, the prophetical books and the historical books thus alike profess to give an authoritative declaration of the will of Jehovah, the sovereign God of Israel.

The reception of these books into the canon was not merely the acknowledgment of their superior excellence and their uplifting spiritual power, but a recognition of the rightfulness of their claim to be a revelation of the will of God. We have already seen (p. 12) that according to the uniform testimony of all the sacred historians, the law of Moses was regarded as divinely obligatory upon Israel at every period of their history. Whatever extent of meaning be given to the expression, " the law of Moses," it is manifest that there was a body of law attributed to him, and believed to be from a divine source which the people and their rulers were bound to obey, and upon the faithful observance of which the prosperity of the nation and its continued existence were dependent. When Josiah and all the people of Judah of all ranks and classes bound themselves by covenant to a steadfast adherence to the book of the law found in the temple in all its requirements, this was not the first sanction given to a law which had never been considered obligatory before, but the recognition of a law of long standing, that was not only binding upon them, but had been equally so upon their fathers, who had incurred serious guilt by transgressing it (2 Kin. xxii. 13), in fact the very law of Moses (xxiii. 25), which their duty to Jehovah required them to keep. This was not the first step toward the formation of a canon, but bowing to an authority coeval with the origin of the nation itself.

And the law which Ezra read to the assembled people, and which by a written and sealed engagement, ratified by an oath they promised to observe, was not, in the intent of Ezra or of the people according to the only record that we have of the transaction, a new book

of the law then for the first time accepted as sacred and
made canonical. It was (Neh. viii. 1) the book of the
law of Moses which Jehovah had commanded to Israel
(ix. 14, x. 29), God's law which was given by Moses the
servant of God, the trangression of which by former
generations had been the cause of all the calamities
which had befallen them (ix. 26, 29, 32–34).

The prophets were recognized expounders of the will
of Jehovah, who were commissioned by him to deliver his messages to the people. And, as we have seen
(p. 17), the prophets are in numerous passages associated with the law, as together constituting the divine standard obligatory upon the people, the disregard of which
brought upon them accumulated evils. Later prophets
also bear abundant testimony to the divine commission
of their predecessors by general statements, as Hos. vi.
5, Jer. vii. 25, by the repetition and enforcement of their
predictions, by citations of their language, or by evident
allusions to them. Thus Ewald:[1] "Even such old
prophets as Amos, Hosea, Isaiah, Micah, like to build
upon the words and writings of older true prophets,
borrow many a passage from them, and many a striking
clause, and refer back to them without mentioning them
by name. Yet in Jeremiah's time appeal was made by
name to the book of Micah, a hundred years before (Jer.
xxvi. 17, 18)." Wildeboer[2] quotes from von Orelli with
approval: "To judge from the citations of older prophets, in younger authors, the writings of an Amos, an
Isaiah, etc., were regarded in a certain sense as holy
scriptures, as the word of God"; and adds, "Of course
as the spoken words of the prophets were the word of
God; they were equally so when committed to writing."
It is evident that the writings of the prophets, as soon

[1] Jahrb. d. Bibl. Wiss., VII., p. 74.
[2] Canon of the Old Testament, p. 123.

as they were issued, would have precisely the same
authority as their discourses orally delivered, and would
be accepted as in precisely the same sense the word of
God. No formal declaration of their canonicity was
needed to give them sanction. They were from the first
not only " eagerly read by the devout," but believed to
be divinely obligatory ; and this without waiting until
there were no more living prophets, and a complete collection could be made of all their writings. Each individual book of an acknowledged prophet of Jehovah, or
of anyone accredited as inspired by him to make known
his will, was accepted as the word of God immediately
upon its appearance. It had its own independent authority, derived from the source from which it came, irrespective of its being united in a collection with the
other books of the same character. And thus the canon
gradually grew, as such books were produced from time
to time, until the last was written, when consequently
the canon was complete.

This view of the formation of the canon is not, as Dillmann supposed, a theological speculation, but a necessary historical deduction. The question with which we
are at present concerned is not as to the reality of the
inspiration of the sacred writers, but as to the faith of
Israel on this subject. Those books, and those only,
were accepted as the divine standards of their faith
and regulative of their conduct which were written for
this definite purpose[1] by those whom they believed to

_____

[1] Books written by inspired men with a different design, or only for
some temporary purpose, and with no claim to divine authority or
permanent obligation, could not, of course, be placed on a par with
their professed divine communications. Expressions in which prophets
simply utter their own thoughts are clearly distinguished from what
they say in the name of God (1 Sam. xvi. 6, 7; 2 Sam. vii. 3, 4, 17).
No record has been preserved of what Solomon spake on subjects of
natural history (1 Kin. iv. 33). Annals of the kingdom, if written by

be inspired of God. It was this which made them canonical. The spiritual profit found in them corresponded with and confirmed the belief in their heavenly origin. And the public official action, which further attested, though it did not initiate, their canonicity, followed in the wake of the popular recognition of their divine authority.[1]

prophets, would have their historical value, even though they might not be in any sense the product of divine inspiration. The same may probably be said of the historical sources referred to in the books of Chronicles (1 Chron. xxix. 29, 30; 2 Chron. ix. 29, xii. 15), which are no longer extant for the reason, doubtless, that they were not intended to form part of the permanent rule of faith. See Alexander on the Canon, pp. 84–93.

[1] "When the Jewish doctors first concerned themselves with the preparation of an authoritative list of sacred books, most of the Old Testament books had already established themselves in the hearts of the faithful with an authority that could neither be shaken nor confirmed by the decision of the schools." Robertson Smith in the Old Testament in the Jewish Church, p. 163.

V

THE COMPLETION OF THE CANON

WE have explicit testimony respecting the time of completing the canon from the Jewish historian Josephus, who was born at Jerusalem, A.D. 37, of priestly descent. In his treatise against Apion, an Alexandrian grammarian, hostile to the Jews, I., 8, he speaks in the following manner of the sacred books: "We have not tens of thousands of books, discordant and conflicting, but only twenty-two, containing the record of all time, which have been justly believed [to be divine [1]]. And of these, five are the books of Moses, which embrace the laws and the tradition from the creation of man until his [Moses'] death. This period is a little short of three thousand years. From the death of Moses to the reign of Artaxerxes, the successor of Xerxes, king of Persia, the prophets who succeeded Moses wrote what was done in thirteen books. The remaining four books embrace hymns to God and counsels for men for the conduct of life. From Artaxerxes until our time everything has been recorded, but has not been deemed worthy of like credit with what preceded, because the exact succession of the prophets ceased. But what faith we have placed in our own writings is evident by our conduct; for though so long a time has now passed, no

[1] Eichhorn (Repertorium f. Bib. u. Morg. Litt., V., p. 254) remarks, "The word 'divine' was not in the old editions of Josephus; it has in recent times been inserted from Eusebius." Later editors are inclined to expunge it.

one has dared either to add anything to them, or to take anything from them, or to alter anything in them. But it is instinctive in all Jews at once from their very birth to regard them as commands of God, and to abide by them, and, if need be, willingly to die for them."

According to Josephus, therefore, the period in which the books esteemed sacred by the Jews were written, extended from the time of Moses to the reign of Artaxerxes I. of Persia; after which no additions of any sort were made to the canon. Artaxerxes Longimanus, the monarch here referred to, reigned forty years, from B.C. 465 to B.C. 425. In the seventh year of his reign Ezra came up to Jerusalem from the captivity (Ezra vii. 1, 8); and in the twentieth year of the same Nehemiah followed him (Neh. ii. 1, 5, 6).

Strenuous efforts have been made to discredit this statement of Josephus, but without good reason. It has been said that it is not based on reliable historical information, nor the general belief of his time, but is merely a private opinion of his own. It is obvious, however, that this cannot be the case. Josephus was a man of considerable learning, and had every facility for acquainting himself with the history of his own nation, upon which he had written largely in his "Antiquities." His priestly origin afforded him special opportunities for becoming familiar with the religious opinions of his countrymen. He is here arguing with a scholar of no mean pretensions, which would naturally make him cautious in his statements; and he gives no intimation that what he here says is simply his own opinion. It is stated as a certain and acknowledged fact. And we have, besides, additional evidence that this was the current belief of his contemporaries. Ryle gives utterance to the common sentiment of scholars, when he says :[1]

---

[1] The Canon of the Old Testament, pp. 162–164.

"We must remember that Josephus writes as the spokesman of his people, in order to defend the accuracy and sufficiency of their Scriptures, as compared with the recent and contradictory histories by Greek writers. In this controversy he defends the judgment of his people. He does not merely express a personal opinion, he claims to represent his countrymen. . . . In the first century A.D. the impression prevailed that the books of the canon were all ancient, that none were more recent than Ahasuerus (Artaxerxes), and that all had long been regarded as canonical."

It is further urged that Josephus makes the mistake of identifying the Artaxerxes of Ezra and Nehemiah with Xerxes ("Antiq.," xi. 5, 1, 6), and the Ahasuerus of Esther with Artaxerxes ("Antiq.," xi. 6, 1), whereas the real fact is the reverse of this. The events related in the book of Esther took place in the reign of Xerxes, and Ezra and Nehemiah lived in the reign of Artaxerxes. It is hence inferred that he regarded Esther as the latest book of the Old Testament, and for this reason makes the reign of Artaxerxes the limit of the canon in the passage quoted above. But it is evident that this error on the part of Josephus does not affect the correctness of his general statement. Whether Esther was prior to Ezra and Nehemiah, or they were prior to Esther, one or the other lived under Artaxerxes, and after his time no book was added to the canon. It is by no means certain, however, that this was in his mind. As the saying was common among the Jews that Malachi was the latest prophet,[1] it is more probable that the time of closing the canon was fixed by the date of his ministry, particularly as the reason given by Josephus himself is

[1] Strack, in Herzog-Plitt Encycl., vii., p. 428, note, quotes from the Talmudic treatise Sanhedrin, "After the latter prophets Haggai, Zechariah, and Malachi, the Holy Spirit departed from Israel."

because then the exact succession of the prophets ceased. As the continuous line of the prophets terminated then, no inspired book could be written afterward.

It does not invalidate Josephus' testimony that he finds sporadic instances of prophetic power at a later time, such as he attributes to John Hyrcanus,[1] who became high priest, B.C. 135, for he has no idea of placing him on a par with the continuous line of prophets who were the authors of the sacred books. He evidently regards him as standing on a much lower plane.

The most serious objection to the truth of Josephus' statement, however, if it could be substantiated, is the allegation that there are books in the Old Testament which were not written until long after the time of Artaxerxes. If this be so, of course it must be acknowledged that Josephus was mistaken. This allegation rests upon critical conclusions which are deduced entirely from certain supposed criteria in the books themselves, but have no external historical support, and are at variance with what has been the generally reputed origin of the books in question. The testimony of Josephus and the common belief of the age in which he lived create a strong presumption against these critical positions, unless some very clear and decisive evidence can be adduced in their favor. As Welte [2] truly says, "The rise of the opinion that with Malachi the Holy Spirit departed from Israel seems incomprehensible, if books acknowledged to be inspired and universally regarded as sacred, which proceeded from a later time, are found in the sacred collection."

---

[1] Antiq., xiii. 10, 7, " He was esteemed by God worthy of the three greatest privileges, the government of his nation, the dignity of the high priesthood, and prophecy, for God was with him, and enabled him to know futurities."

[2] Theologische Quartalschrift, 1855, p. 83.

It will not be possible here to enter upon a full discussion of the date of the books of Chronicles, Ezra, Nehemiah, Ecclesiastes, Esther, and Daniel, which the critics contend were not written until after the time of Artaxerxes. It will be sufficient for our present purpose to examine briefly the grounds upon which this contention rests, as they are stated by Dr. Driver in his "Literature of the Old Testament."

Of Chronicles he says, p. 518: "The only positive clue which the book contains as to the date at which it was composed is the genealogy in 1 Chron. iii. 17–24, which (if ver. 21 be rightly interpreted) is carried down to the *sixth* generation after Zerubbabel. This would imply a date not earlier than *cir.* 350 B.C.; iii. 21, is, however, obscurely expressed ; and it is doubtful if the text is correct." And he adds in a note that if the rendering of the LXX., Pesh., Vulg. be adopted, it will bring down the genealogy to the *eleventh* generation after Zerubbabel.

The actual fact is that Zerubbabel's descendants are traced in iii. 19–21a for two generations only, viz.: Zerubbabel, Hananiah, Pelatiah. There are then added, in a disconnected manner, four separate families, whose origin and relation to the preceding are not stated, and one of these families is traced through four generations ; but there is no intimation whatever that this family or either of the others belonged in the line of descent from Zerubbabel. They were, doubtless, families known at the time who belonged, in a general way, among the descendants of David, which is the subject of the entire chapter. But their particular line of descent is not indicated. That by gratuitously assuming them to be sprung from Zerubbabel six generations can be counted, or eleven by a conjectural alteration of the text in the manner of the ancient versions, is no secure basis for the conclusion that the book belongs to a later date than has always hitherto been believed.

Dr. Driver tells us that " more conclusive evidence is afforded by the books of Ezra and Nehemiah, which certainly belong to the same age, and are commonly assumed to be the work of the same compiler." As we are not concerned at present about the internal constitution of these books, but simply with the question whether they are posterior in date to the reign of Artaxerxes, we pass over the alleged "indications of their compilatory character," and proceed to consider the "marks of their having been compiled in an age long subsequent to that of Ezra and Nehemiah," p. 545. These are thus stated :

a. " The phrase ' King of Persia " (Ezra i. 1, 2, 8, iii. 7, iv. 2, 3, 7, 24, vii. 1) ; the addition would, during the period of the Persian supremacy, be at once unnecessary and contrary to contemporary usage; the expression used by Ezra and Nehemiah, when speaking in their own person (Ezra vii. 27 f., viii. 1, 22, 25, 36; Neh. i. 11, ii. 1 ff., 18 f., v. 4, 14, vi. 7, xiii. 6), or in passages extracted from sources written under the Persian rule (Ezra iv. 8, 11, 17, 23, v. 6 f., 13 f., 17, vi. 1, 3, 13, 15, vii. 7, 11, 21; Neh. xi. 23, 24) is simply ' the king.' " In a note on the next page it is added, " Persia was absorbed and lost in the wider empire of which by Cyrus' conquest of Babylon the Achamenidæ became the heirs ; hence after that date their standing official title is not ' King of Persia,' but ' King of Babylon,' or more commonly the King, the great King, King of kings, King of the lands, etc."

But (1) the assumption that the Persian monarchs are in the book of Ezra simply called "the King " by contemporaries, and that the phrase "King of Persia " indicates a late compiler, will not account for the facts of the case. For both designations occur together in contexts incapable of division; thus "Cyrus the king," i. 7, but "King of Persia," vs. 1, 2, 8, "Artaxerxes the king," vii. 7, but "King of Persia," ver. 1.[1]

(2) If i. 2 has preserved the language of Cyrus' edict, he calls himself "King of Persia," as he is likewise entitled in the inscription of Nabuna'id, the last king of Babylon. It is argued that its "Jewish phraseology and Jewish point of view" disprove its "literal exactness." But it is no more surprising that Cyrus should ascribe his victories to Jehovah and promise to aid in building his temple in a proclamation freeing the Jews, than that he should seek to ingratiate himself with the people upon his entry into Babylon by attributing his successes and his universal empire to Merodach, the patron-god of that city, and declaring himself his worshipper, and inscribing his name on bricks as "builder of Esakkil and Ezida," the temples of Merodach and Nebo. It is true that of the few inscriptions of Cyrus thus far discovered there is no one in which he styles himself "King of Persia"; but this casts no suspicion upon the accuracy of this record in Ezra. Darius twice entitles himself "King of Persia," in his Behistun inscription, though this title has not yet been found upon any other of his inscriptions. Why may not Cyrus have done the same thing in this one instance? and for the reason that while the title "King of Babylon" was in the experience of the Jews associated only with oppression and injury, they were prepared to hail as their deliverer the "King of Persia," by whom their enemy was overthrown.

[1] If vi. 13-15 is copied from a document written before the arrival of Ezra, Dr. Driver is right in his contention that "Artaxerxes king of Persia" is a subsequent addition; otherwise this is another example of the combination of both phrases.

(3) In the letters to Artaxerxes (iv. 8–23) and to and from Darius (v. 6–vi. 13), these monarchs are simply called "the king." Artaxerxes is called "the king" in the Book of Nehemiah, and in that of Ezra after vii. 1. But in the narrative prior to the coming of Ezra the title "King of Persia" is repeatedly applied to Cyrus, Darius, and Artaxerxes. Now it is said that after the conquest of Babylon, Cyrus and his successors assumed the title "King of Babylon," which is given them (Ezra v. 13; Neh. xiii. 6; cf. Ezra vi. 22 "King of Assyria"); but the title "King of Persia" implies a writer subsequent to "the period of the Persian supremacy." This seems to be a sweeping conclusion from very slender premises. If Darius could call himself "King of Persia," as he does in his Behistun inscription, and Cyrus give himself the same title, as is attested (Ezra i. 2), and there is no good reason for discrediting, why might they not be so called by others? It is said that after the fall of the Persian empire its monarchs were called "kings of Persia" in distinction from the Greek kings who succeeded them. A precisely similar reason applies to the Jewish exiles on their first return to Jerusalem. It was natural for them to speak of the "kings of Persia" who had freed them from exile in distinction from the kings of Babylon who had carried them into exile (Ezra ii. 1); in distinction likewise from their own native princes the kings of Israel (iii. 10). They were no longer under kings reigning in Jerusalem, as their fathers had been, but under foreign domination (Neh. ix. 36, 37), which was a distressing situation, even though they were ruled by a friendly power, "the kings of Persia," as Ezra himself calls them (ix. 9, see ver. 5), which is of itself a sufficient refutation of the critical contention.

b. "Neh. xii. 11, 22 Jaddua, three generations later

than Eliashib, the contemporary of Nehemiah, high priest B.C. 351–331, is mentioned."

c. "Neh. xii. 22 'Darius the Persian' must (from the context) be Darius Codomannus, the last king of Persia, B.C. 336–332; and the title 'the Persian' could only have become a distinctive one after the Persian period was past."

As Jaddua was high priest at the time of the invasion of Asia by Alexander the Great,[1] and his victory over Darius Codomannus, it would appear as though these verses indicate a date nearly or quite a century after Artaxerxes Longimanus. From this the critics infer that the books of Chronicles, Ezra, and Nehemiah must all be referred to a compiler living at this late period.

But (1) this conclusion is much too broad for the premise on which it is built. The Book of Nehemiah is preceded (i. 1) by a title of its own referring it to him as its author. And, as Keil remarks, its being counted with Ezra as together forming one book in early lists of the canon no more establishes unity of authorship than the fact that the twelve Minor Prophets were reckoned one book in the same lists proves that they had a common author. A conclusion with regard to the date of Nehemiah, if well founded, would have no bearing upon the determination of the age of the books of Ezra and Chronicles.

(2) It is further to be observed that the list of priests and Levites in xii. 1–26 is a section complete in itself, and with no very close connection either with what precedes or follows.[2] The utmost that the critical argument of date could prove, if its validity were confessed,

---

[1] Josephus, Ant., xi. 8, 4.

[2] It is not wholly unconnected, for the introduction of this list at this place appears to be due to the prominent part taken by priests and Levites in the dedication of the wall of Jerusalem, vs. 27–43.

would be that this section could not have been a pre-existing document, which Nehemiah inserted in the body of his narrative, as he did the similar list in vii. 5b ff. If xii. 1–26 really contained internal evidence of belonging to a century after the time of Nehemiah, this would not invalidate his authorship of the rest of the book, in which no indication of late date is to be found. It would merely show that this section did not belong to the book as originally written, but was a subsequent interpolation.[1]

(3) If, however, xii. 1–26 be examined more closely, it will be found that the condemnation of even this passage is more than the critical argument will justify. The section begins (vs. 1–9) with " the priests and the Levites that went up with Zerubbabel and Jeshua." It proceeds (vs. 12–21) with the priests " in the days of Joiakim " the son of Jeshua. Then follow (vs. 24, 25) "the chiefs of the Levites," concluding with the words (ver. 26), " these were in the days of Joiakim, the son of Jeshua, and in the days of Nehemiah the governor, and Ezra the priest the scribe." This is accordingly a tabular statement of the priests and Levites, including both those who came up with the first colony of exiles under Zerubbabel and Jeshua, and those of a subsequent generation, who lived during the high priesthood of Joiakim, the son of Jeshua, and were contemporaries of Ezra and Nehemiah. This being the declared design of this section, one of two things must follow, either vs. 10, 11, and vs. 22, 23 do not have the meaning attributed to them by the critics, or else they are out of harmony with the section in which they are found, and so are no proper part of it. Each of these alternatives has had its advocates.

[1] This is maintained among others by Bertholdt, Einleitung, III., p. 1031, and Prideaux, The Old and New Testament Connected, i., p. 252.

(1.) Hävernick[1] endeavors to show without much success that Nehemiah might have lived until Jaddua became High Priest. Keil relieves the matter by remarking that ver. 11 merely traces the line of descent to Jaddua, without attributing to him any official position; and even ver. 22, "Levites in the days of Eliashib, Joiada, Johanan, and Jaddua," need not be intended to embrace four distinct bodies of Levites, living severally under one or other of four different high priests, but a single body of men with whom these four generations of sacerdotal rank were contemporaries, Eliashib in advanced age, his great-grandson Jaddua in early youth. According to xiii. 28, Nehemiah expelled a grandson of Eliashib, who had married a daughter of Sanballat. It is, therefore, quite supposable that he lived to see Jaddua, the great-grandchild of Eliashib. The adjustment of this hypothesis to other known facts only requires that Nehemiah, who came to Jerusalem B.C. 444, when perhaps twenty years of age, and Jaddua, who lived until the visit of Alexander, B.C. 332, could have been contemporaries for say eighteen years. If each of them attained the age of seventy-five, which is surely no violent supposition, the period is covered.[2]

[1] Einleitung, II., i., pp. 320–322.

[2] There is much uncertainty in regard to the terms of office of the high priests after the return from exile in consequence of the conflicting statements of authorities. See Herzfeld, Geschichte, II., Excursus xi., p. 368. Keil needlessly infers from Neh. xiii. 4, 7, that Eliashib died between Nehemiah's return to the king in the thirty-second year of Artaxerxes, B.C. 433, and his second visit to Jerusalem. Then supposing Jaddua to be ten years old at the time of his great-grandfather's death, he would have been one hundred and ten when Alexander came to Jerusalem, to which he compares Jehoiada, high priest under king Joash, living to the age of one hundred and thirty (2 Chron. xxiv. 15). But if with Prideaux, i., p. 321, the death of Eliashib is put twenty years later, B.C. 413, Jaddua would on the same supposition have been ninety when he met Alexander.

The inference "from the context" that the Darius of Neh. xii. 22b is Darius Codomannus, is based on the assumption that in ver. 22a Jaddua is spoken of as high priest. If, on the other hand, his boyhood is intended, Darius Nothus, B.C. 424–405, would be meant. The assertion that "the title 'the Persian' could only have become a distinctive one after the Persian period was past," is contradicted by the Nakshi-Rustan inscription of Darius Hystaspes, which in recording his foreign possessions calls him " a Persian, son of a Persian," and speaks of him as the " Persian man who fought battles far from his land Persia." The significance of the title lies in his bearing rule over non-Persian lands, not in distinguishing him from a non-Persian successor.

(2.) If, however, in vs. 10, 11, 22, 23, Jaddua is regarded as high priest, and Darius Codomannus is intended, these verses cannot properly belong in a list, which limits itself to " the priests and Levites that went up with Zerubbabel and Jeshua," and those who were "in the days of Joiakim, Nehemiah, and Ezra." They must have been added at a later time to extend the list beyond its original dimensions. Eichhorn [1] truly says : " That these are a foreign addition by a later hand can not only be made probable, but as rigidly proved as can ever be expected in regard to books so ancient and with critical aids so recent. The contents of these verses destroys the unity of the entire chapter, and presents something that the author did not mean to give. They give a genealogy of the high priests from Jeshua onward ; and no other passage in this chapter is genealogical." Dr. Driver refers in a footnote to this ready reply to the alleged indication of late date, but adds " even supposing this to have been the case, the other

[1] Einleitung, 4th edition, III., p. 631.

marks of late composition which the books contain would still remain." We shall see whether there is any more force in "the other marks" than in this which he seems willing to surrender.

d. " Neh. xii. 26, 47, the 'days of Nehemiah' are spoken of in terms clearly implying that the writer looked back upon them as past."

" The days of Nehemiah " is manifestly an expression that could be used indifferently by a contemporary of Nehemiah, or by one who lived subsequent to his time. There is nothing in the expression itself or in the connection in which it stands to give the preference to the latter alternative. The famous men and the remarkable events that have added lustre to the reign of Queen Victoria can be spoken of without implying that her beneficent reign is ended.

e. " Other indications of the same fact will appear below ; *e.g.*, the position of Ezra iv. 6–23 (which referring, as it does, to what happened under Xerxes and Artaxerxes, could not possibly have been placed where it now stands by Ezra, a *contemporary* of the latter), the contents and character of vii. 1–10," etc.

First as to iv. 6–23. Ch. iv. 1–5 opens with an account of the vexatious conduct of the Samaritans, who, when their proffered aid was declined in building the temple, obstructed the work in every possible way during the entire reign of Cyrus, and until the reign of Darius Hystaspes, who held their hostility in check for a time. Before explaining the action of Darius in this matter the author proceeds to tell how this hostility broke out afresh in the beginning of the very next reign, that of Ahasuerus (=Xerxes, ver. 6), and in the following reign succeeded in obtaining from Artaxerxes an edict forbidding the construction of the city walls (vs. 7–23). The writer then reverts to the first stage of this hostility (ver. 5), the stoppage of the work upon the temple, and relates in detail how the favor of Darius was secured, and how effectually he thwarted the designs of the Samaritans (iv. 24–vi. 15), an intimation being given (vi. 14) of an edict of Artaxerxes of a different tenor from that first issued, without explaining how it was brought about. The way is now prepared for the mission of Ezra and his reformatory labors (Ezra vii.–x.) and for that of Nehemiah, to whom it was left to explain how the favor of Artaxerxes was obtained, and how he was induced to give orders for the rebuilding of the walls (Neh. i., ii.).

Opinions may differ as to the wisdom of the plan which the writer has seen fit to adopt. I agree with those who think it carefully considered and well carried out. Dr. Driver and others are utterly dissatisfied with it. They complain that " the notice of the letter to Ahasuerus and the correspondence with Artaxerxes relate to a different and subsequent period, and is out of place, as they relate to the interruptions to the project of rebuilding, not the temple, but the city walls, occurrences some eighty years later than the period he was describing." The writer might, indeed, if he had so chosen, upon the mention of the interruptions to the rebuilding of the temple, have proceeded at once to say how these were overcome and when the temple was completed, and have reserved the obstruction to the rebuilding of the walls to a later point in his narrative. But it was equally consistent with good style to group together the successive acts of hostility which the Jews experienced from their neighbors, and let the progress of the history show how the temple and the walls of Jerusalem were finally built in spite of all that their enemies could do to prevent it. In this there is no overleaping a period of " eighty years." The trouble is

traced through each successive reign : in ver. 5, Cyrus
to Darius ; then ver. 6, Xerxes ; then ver. 7, Artaxerxes
There is no good reason for the charge that this is a
method which could only mislead and confuse the
reader." And the mistake attributed to the writer of
referring " to troubles connected with the restoration
of the temple what related in fact to the restoration of
the city walls " really belongs to those interpreters who,
disregarding the plain sense of the language used, en-
deavored to force it into correspondence with preconceived notions of their own.

Secondly, as to vii. 1–10. It is claimed on very trivial
grounds that this " is certainly not Ezra's work," but
none of the objections which are raised have the sem-
blance of implying a later date than the time of Ezra.
Notice is taken of " the omission of Ezra's immediate
ancestors (for Seraiah was contemporary with Zedekiah,
2 Kin. xxv. 18–21), one hundred and thirty years previously to Ezra's time." The only inference which can
be drawn from this is that Ezra preferred to link himself
with his distinguished ancestors before the exile rather
than with those since of less note. He was sprung
from the line of high priests extending from Aaron to
Seraiah, but not including Jehozadak, Seraiah's successor (1 Chron. vi. 14, 15), the probability being that he
was descended from a younger son of Seraiah, so that
the family was thenceforward of lower rank.

" Vs. 7–9 anticipate ch. viii." In introducing himself to his readers Ezra first gives his pedigree (vs. 1–5),
then states very briefly and in general terms the fact,
the purpose, and the time of his coming to Jerusalem
with a fresh colony of exiles (vs. 6–10), as preliminary
to a detailed account of his commission from the king
(vs. 11–28), the persons who accompanied him (viii.
1–14), and the particulars of the expedition (vs. 15–31)

and its arrival (vs. 32–36). It is difficult to see why the same person might not write all this continuously.

"The expressions of the compiler in ver. 10," the evidence of which is found in their correspondence with expressions in the Books of Chronicles. But what if the compiler was Ezra himself, who has very generally been supposed to be the author of Chronicles? And Dr. Driver admits that he uses one of Ezra's expressions at the end of vs. 6, 9. Whether, however, Ezra wrote the book which bears his name, or it was compiled by another, is of little moment so far as our present inquiry is concerned, unless it can be shown that the compilation was made after Ezra's own time.

Thirdly. One more argument remains : "There are long periods on which the narrative is silent; in one case especially (Ezra vi. 22–vii. 1), an interval of sixty years, *immediately before Ezra's own time*, being passed over by the words 'After these things' in a manner not creditable if the writer were Ezra himself, but perfectly natural if the writer lived in an age to which the period, B.C. 516–458, was visible only in a distant perspective." It should be remembered, however, that the book does not profess to be an annalistic record of all that took place. It deals with the early condition and prospects of the infant colony and the progress made in re-establishing the worship of God, and in freeing the people from heathenish contamination ; and periods in which there was nothing to record which was germane to the purpose of the writer are, of course, passed over slightly. " After these things " (vii. 1) refers not only to the dedication of the temple fifty-eight years before, as described in the immediately preceding verses, but to all that had been previously recorded, including (iv.

6–23) the embarrassments which had arisen in the reign of Xerxes and Artaxerxes almost at the very time of Ezra's coming.

The arguments adduced to prove that the books of Chronicles, Ezra, and Nehemiah belong to "a date shortly after B.C. 333," when the Persian empire was overthrown by Alexander the Great, have now been examined, and it is fair to say that so far from establishing the date alleged, they point to nothing later than the age of Ezra and Nehemiah, or the close of the reign of Artaxerxes, B.C. 425.

The only data for ascertaining the age of the Book of Ecclesiastes are its reflections upon governmental abuses and the character of its language; and these are of too vague and general a nature to lead to a determinate result.   Dr. Driver says ("Lit. O. T.," p. 471) : "Its pages reflect the depression produced by the corruption of an Oriental despotism, with its injustice (iii. 16, iv. 1, v. 8, viii. 9), its capriciousness (x. 5f.), its revolutions (x. 7), its system of spies (x. 20), its hopelessness of reform. Its author must have lived when the Jews had lost their national independence and formed but a province of the Persian empire, perhaps even later when they had passed under the rule of the Greeks (3d cent. B.C.)." And (p. 475f.) "The *precise* date of Ecclesiastes cannot be determined, our knowledge of the history not enabling us to interpret with any confidence the allusions to concrete events which it seems to contain.   But the general political condition which it presupposes, and the language, make it decidedly probable that it is not earlier than the latter years of the Persian rule, which ended B.C. 333, and it is quite possible that it is later." How inconclusive this argument is in Dr. Driver's own esteem is apparent from the use made of "perhaps," "probable," and "possible" in the course of it. Doubt-

less any Oriental despotism, Babylonish, Persian, or
Grecian, at any period of its history, would afford abundant materials for just such reflections as are to be
found in Ecclesiastes. And for all that appears they
could be indulged in the first century of the Persian
domination, B.C. 536–436, as well as afterward.

Dr. Driver further says (p. 473) : "Linguistically,
Ecclesiastes stands by itself in the Old Testament. The
Hebrew in which it is written has numerous features in
common with the latest parts of the Old Testament,
Ezra and Nehemiah, Chronicles, Esther, but it has in
addition many not met with in these books, but found
first in the Mishnah (which includes, no doubt, older
elements, but received its present form cir. 200 A.D.).
The characteristic of the Hebrew in which these latest
parts of the Old Testament are written is that while
many of the old classical words and expressions still
continue in use, and, in fact, still preponderate, the syntax is deteriorated, the structure of sentences is cum-
brous and inelegant, and there is a very decided admix-
ture of words and idioms not found before, having
usually affinities with the Aramaic, or being such as are
in constant and regular use in the Hebrew of post-
Christian times (the Mishnah, etc.). And this latter
element is decidedly larger and more prominent in
Ecclesiastes than in either Esther or Ezra, Nehemiah,
Chronicles." And (p. 476) some "place it cir. 200 B.C.
on the ground of language, which *favors,* even though
our knowledge is not sufficient to enable us to say that
it *requires,* a date later than" the latter years of the Persian rule.

But in the chaotic condition of the Hebrew language
after the exile, and its rapid deterioration from constant
contact with the Aramean, from which it had already received a large infusion, and which was in familiar use

along with it, as is shown by the Aramean sections of
the Book of Ezra, the measure of its degeneracy in any
particular writing cannot afford a certain criterion of its
relative date.   The critics certainly do not feel themselves bound by any such rule.   The purity of Joel's
style does not prevent them from attempting to prove
him postexilic.   They do not hesitate to place Isaiah
xl.-lxvi., notwithstanding its classic elegance, later than
Ezekiel with his abundant Aramaisms and anomalous
forms.   The Hebrew original of the Book of Sirach or
Ecclesiasticus is, in the judgment of Dr. Driver (p. 474
note), predominantly classical, " and in syntax and
general style stands upon a much higher level than Ecclesiastes or Esther, Ezra, Nehemiah, Chronicles," all of
which he places a century or more before it.   In our
ignorance of the extent to which the popular language
had been corrupted by Aramaisms in the first century
after the exile, or how far the language of certain books
written at that time may have been affected by the imitation of earlier models, it cannot with any show of reason be affirmed that such a book as Ecclesiastes could
not have been produced then.

The attempt to establish a late date for the book by
the supposed detection of Sadducean sentiments or of
the influence of certain forms of Greek philosophy has
still less to recommend it.

In regard to Esther, Dr. Driver says (p. 484) : " Materials do not exist for fixing otherwise than approxi-
mately the date at which the Book of Esther was composed.   Xerxes is described (i. 1f.) in terms which imply that his reign lay in a somewhat distant past when
the author wrote.   By the majority of critics the book
is assigned either to the early years of the Greek period
(which began B.C. 332), or to the third century B.C.
With such a date the diction would well agree, which,

though superior to that of the Chronicler, and more accommodated to the model of the earlier historical books, contains many late words and idioms, and exhibits much deterioration in syntax."

No protracted period after the reign of Xerxes is required to account for the manner in which he is spoken of (i. 1 f.). The language used would be entirely appropriate under his immediate successor Artaxerxes Longimanus. And the character of the Hebrew of the Book of Esther finds an adequate explanation then as well as at a later time. The critical opinion, which would place it one or two centuries later, is due to a disposition to discredit the history, which accords admirably with what is known from other sources of the life and character of Xerxes, and of Persian customs, and is confirmed by the feast of Purim, established in commemoration of the deliverance here recorded, and which, according to Josephus,[1] the Jews have observed ever since.

Of all the revolutionary conclusions of the critics there is no one that is affirmed with greater positiveness or with an air of more assured confidence than that the Book of Daniel is a product of the Maccabean period. And yet Delitzsch,[2] before he had himself yielded to the prevailing current, correctly describes it as a book, " which has been of the most commanding and most effective influence on the New Testament writings, which belongs to the most essential presuppositions of the Apocalypse of John, and to the predictions of which He who is the way, the truth, and the life for science also, attaches an emphatic Nota Bene (let him that readeth understand Mat. xxiv. 15); a book, the genuineness of which had no other opposer for almost two thousand years than the heathen scoffer Porphyry in his ' Words

---

[1] Ant., xi. 6, 12.   [2] Herzog's Encyklopædie, III., p. 271.

against Christians,' but whose spuriousness has in Germany, since Semler and Eichhorn, become step by step a more and more indubitable fact to the Biblical Criticism which proceeds from rationalistic presuppositions. . . . The principal ground of modern Criticism against its genuineness, as it makes no concealment whatever itself, lies in the miracles and predictions of the book." With almost unbroken uniformity the critics unhesitatingly determine the date of the book by what they consider the limit of its professed predictions, which in their esteem are merely history in the garb of prophecy.

Dr. Driver indeed makes a show of separating the literary from the dogmatic grounds on which it is claimed that the book is not "the work of Daniel himself." According to Dr. Driver, "Internal evidence shows, with a cogency that cannot be resisted, that it must have been written not earlier than circ. 300 B.C., and in Palestine; and it is at least probable that it was composed under the persecution of Antiochus Epiphanes, 168 or 167 B.C.

"1. The following are facts of a historical nature, which point more or less decisively to an author later than Daniel himself:

"a. The position of the book in the Jewish Canon, not among the prophets, but in the miscellaneous collection of writings called the *Hagiographa*, and among the latest of these, in proximity to Esther. Though little definite is known respecting the formation of the Canon, the division known as the 'Prophets,' was doubtless formed prior to the Hagiographa; and had the Book of Daniel existed at the time, it is reasonable to suppose that it would have ranked as the work of a prophet, and have been included among the former."

The fact is that its being included in the Canon is a

serious obstacle to the critical hypothesis of its late date. And as will be shown, when we come to consider the threefold division of the Canon, it has its proper place, and that not in conflict with but confirmatory of the date which it claims for itself and which has until recent times been uniformly attributed to it.

"*b.* Jesus, the son of Sirach (writing circ. 200 B.C.), in his enumeration of Israelitish worthies, ch. xliv.-l., though he mentions Isaiah, Jeremiah, Ezekiel and (collectively) the twelve Minor Prophets, is silent as to Daniel."

So, too, though he mentions Zerubbabel, Jeshua the son of Jozadak, and Nehemiah, he is silent as to Ezra. Are we, therefore, to infer that there was no such person as Ezra, or that he was not associated with Nehemiah, or that he was of so little consequence that the son of Sirach had never heard of him? And shall the silence of the son of Sirach outweigh the express mention of Daniel by his contemporary Ezekiel (xiv. 14, 20, xxviii. 3)?[1]

"*c.* That Nebuchadnezzar besieged Jerusalem and

---

[1] Dr. Driver says, p. 510 note: "Whether he is alluded to in Ezek. xiv. 14, 20, xxviii. 3 is uncertain: the terms in which Ezekiel speaks in ch. xiv., seem to suggest a patriarch of antiquity, rather than a younger contemporary of his own." The remark is gratuitous and without the slightest foundation. "Noah, Daniel, and Job" are grouped together, with no reference to the age in which they lived, as signal instances of those who had delivered others by their righteousness; Noah, whose family were saved with himself from the flood; Daniel, who by his prevailing prayer rescued the wise men of Babylon from being slain by the frenzied order of the king (Dan. ii. 18-24); and Job, whose three friends were spared at his intercession (Job xlii. 7-9). If Grant, Julius Cæsar, and Alexander the Great were mentioned together as three famous generals, would the fact that one was modern and the others ancient make the identity of the first named uncertain? The Daniel of the captivity precisely answers to Ezekiel's description, and there is no other that does.

carried away some of the sacred vessels in 'the *third* year of Jehoiakim' (Dan. i. 1 f.), though it cannot, strictly speaking, be disproved, is highly improbable; not only is the Book of Kings silent, but Jeremiah, *in the following year* (ch. xxv., etc.; see ver. 1), speaks of the Chaldeans in a manner which appears distinctly to imply that their arms had not yet been seen in Judah."

The solution of this imaginary difficulty is very simple. It is only necessary to remember that a military expedition is not always finished in the same year in which it is undertaken. Nebuchadnezzar began his march in the third year of Jehoiakim. His advance was disputed by Pharaoh-neco; the decisive battle of Carchemish, which broke the power of Egypt, was fought in the fourth year of Jehoiakim (Jer. xlvi. 1). The way was now clear for Nebuchadnezzar to continue his march and lay siege to Jerusalem. The Hebrew verb in Dan. i. 1 does not require us to understand that Nebuchadnezzar arrived in Jerusalem in the third year of Jehoiakim, much less that he finished his siege and carried off his booty in that year. It is the same verb that is used of the vessel, in which Jonah took passage (Jon. i. 3), which was not then arriving in Tarshish, but "going to Tarshish," *i.e.*, setting out on its voyage to that place.

"*d.* The 'Chaldeans' are synonymous in Dan. i. 4, ii. 2, etc., with the caste of wise men. This sense 'is unknown in the Ass.-Bab. language, has, wherever it occurs, formed itself after the end of the Babylonian empire, and is thus an indication of the post-exilic composition of the book' (Schrader, Keilinschriften und d. A. Test., Ed. 2, p. 429). It dates, namely, from a time when practically the only 'Chaldeans' known belonged to the caste in question."

One might naturally suppose from the positive manner in which this assertion is made, that all the senses which the word "Chaldeans" had or could have in the language of Babylon were well known, and that it was an ascertained fact that a meaning is attributed to it in the Book of Daniel which was entirely foreign to Babylonish usage. And yet Schrader himself says (p. 133 of the very volume from which the above assertion is taken), "that the name Chaldeans has thus far only been found in Assyrian monuments," and that "hitherto we possess accounts about the Chaldeans only from Assyrian sources"; so that, while it is conjectured that the Babylonish pronunciation of the word has been preserved in the Hebrew, as the Assyrian has in the Greek, even this is as yet without monumental verification. It would appear, therefore, that he had no monumental authority whatever for saying that the word "Chaldeans" was not applied in Babylon, as it is in the Book of Daniel, to one of the classes of wise men.

" e. Belshazzar is represented as king of Babylon; and Nebuchadnezzar is spoken of throughout ch. v. (vs. 2, 11, 13, 18, 22) as his *father*. In point of fact Nabonidus (Nabunahid) was the last king of Babylon; he was a usurper, not related to Nebuchadnezzar, and one *Belsharuzur* is mentioned as his son."

It is surprising that this notable proof of the writer's familiarity with affairs in Babylon should be urged as an objection to Daniel's authorship. No ancient writer, native or foreign, has preserved the name of Belshazzar, or given any hint of his existence, except the Book of Daniel. Daniel's Belshazzar was accordingly a puzzle to believers in the authenticity of the book, and a butt of ridicule to unbelievers, like Isaiah's casual mention of Sargon (xx. 1), who is similarly unknown to any other ancient writer. But the first Assyrian mound excavated by Botta proved to be the palace of Sargon, and Isaiah was vindicated. Nabuna'id's Sippara inscription solved the mystery of Belshazzar, of whom he speaks as " his eldest son, the offspring of his heart." "Belshazzar the king's son" is likewise spoken of in several contract tablets in connection with his household arrangements and business transactions in which he was concerned. From the annalistic inscription of Nabuna'id, which records his movements in each successive year of his reign, it appears that Belshazzar was in command of the troops in northern Babylonia, while Nabuna'id himself remained in Tema, a suburb of Babylon, from his seventh to his eleventh year. There is then an unfortunate break in the inscription until Nabuna'id's last year, his seventeenth, when he is stated to have been himself at the head of the troops in northern Babylonia to resist the advance of Cyrus, and was defeated by him. This creates the presumption that Belshazzar may have been on duty elsewhere, perhaps in charge of the capital, which would be in accord with Dan. v.

But Dr. Driver insists that "the inscriptions lend no support to the hypothesis that Belsharuzur was his father's viceroy, or was entitled to be spoken of as ' king'; he was called 'the king's son' to the day of his death." According to the inscriptions Belshazzar was the king's son, his first born, his dearly beloved son, and in command of the army ; what is there in this to discredit the additional statement of the Book of Daniel that he was addressed as "king "? or to forbid the assumption that he may have been formally raised to the dignity of participation with his father in the kingdom, perhaps in those later years of his reign, the record of which in the annalistic inscription has been unfortunately obliterated? In the first edition of his " Literature of the Old Testament " Dr. Driver says, in a footnote, "In respect of vii. 1, viii. 1, if they stood alone, *association with his father on the throne would be conceivable*. But in v. 28, 30 he *seems* to be described as sole king." The statement in the first sentence covers the entire case. The affirmation in the second sentence is a most extraordinary one, inasmuch as v. 29 makes it evident that Belshazzar was not sole king. Why was Daniel promoted to be the *third* ruler in the kingdom? Why not *second*, as in the case of Joseph, who was advanced to be next to Pharaoh? This was never understood until the position of Belshazzar was cleared up by the monuments. Daniel was third because next to Nabuna'id and Belshazzar. Dr. Driver's suggestion, p. 490, that Daniel was "made one of the three chief ministers in the kingdom," like the marginal rendering of the English Revisers, "rule as one of three," is a simple evasion and a departure from the plain meaning of the original word.

But how could Nebuchadnezzar be the father of Belshazzar, when his real father was Nabuna'id, "a usurper, not related to Nebuchadnezzar"? Here Dr. Driver makes the reluctant admission : "There remains the *possibility* that Nabu-nahid may have sought to strengthen his position by marrying a daughter of Nebuchadnezzar, in which case the latter might be spoken of as Belshazzar's father (= grandfather, by Hebrew usage). The terms of ch. v., however, produce certainly the impression that, in the view of the writer, Belshazzar was actually Neb.'s son." It might as well be said that when Jesus is called "the son of David," the view of the writer must have been that he was David's immediate descendant. These words might be so interpreted by one who did not know from other sources that this could not be their meaning. We have, it is true, no positive information that Nabuna'id was thus allied with the family of Nebuchadnezzar; but there are corroborating circumstances, which, to say the least, heighten the "possibility" into a very strong probability. This supposition is commended by its perfectly reconciling all the statements in the case; such a marriage may have inflamed his ambition and led to his usurpation after the example of Neriglissar, the successful conspirator against his brother-in-law Evil-merodach, the son of Nebuchadnezzar; this, too, explains the fact, attested by the Behistun inscription, that Nabuna'id had a son Nebuchadnezzar, who was twice personated by impostors in the reign of Darius Hystaspes. My colleague, Dr. Davis, has called my attention to an unpublished coronation inscription [1] of Nabuna'id, in which he says: "Of Nebuchadnezzar and Neriglissar the kings my predecessors their mighty descendant I am he." This explicit claim on the part of Nabuna'id, however he may have justified it, is direct monumental evidence that he, and by consequence also his son Belshazzar, considered themselves descendants of Nebuchadnezzar.

One mutilated passage in the annalistic inscription, which is understood by Sayce, Schrader, and Winckler to record the death of "the king's wife," has more recently been translated by Hagen, with the approval of Pinches and Frederick Delitzsch, "On the night of the eleventh of Marchesvan Gobryas attacked and killed the son (?) of the king." Upon which Dr. Driver remarks: "When the Persians (as the same inscription shows) had been in peaceable possession of Babylon for *four months*, how could Belshazzar, even supposing (what is not in itself inconceivable) that he still held out in the palace, and was slain afterward in attempting to defend it, promise and dispense (v. 7, 16, 29) honors in his kingdom, and what need could there be for the solemn announcement

[1] Translated in part by Boscawen, Biblical and Oriental Record, September, 1896.

(v. 25-28), as of something new and unexpected, that his (or his father's) kingdom was to be given to the Medes and Persians, when it must have been patent to everyone that they were already in possession of it?"

It is scarcely necessary to take any special pains to defend the accuracy of the Book of Daniel against this hypothetical rendering, of which Hagen himself says: "It is greatly to be regretted that the words which give account of the death which took place in the night of the eleventh of Marchesvan, have come down to us so mutilated and defaced. . . . Before a decisive utterance can be made on a point so unusually important historically, it is necessary to wait for a duplicate of the text, which shall leave no doubt whatever as to the characters in question." But supposing the case to be precisely as Dr. Driver puts it, it will be observed that the inscription so understood confirms the account of Daniel in at least three important particulars, viz., that Belshazzar met a violent death, in the night, and on the final collapse of the Babylonish power. The difficulties suggested by Dr. Driver will be dispelled, if Belshazzar and his lords believed the palace impregnable, and cherished the expectation that their armies might yet be rallied and the intruder expelled. It has its parallels in Jeremiah's purchase of a field in Anathoth at the very time that Jerusalem was besieged by Nebuchadnezzar and the captivity was imminent (Jer. xxxii. 8-12); and in the public sale by Romans of the land on which Hannibal was encamped, while he was thundering at the gates of their city with every prospect of accomplishing its overthrow.

Dr. Driver sums up the whole situation, as he regards it, in the words, "The historical presuppositions of Dan. v. are inconsistent with the evidence of the contemporary monuments." On the contrary, a careful exam-

ination of all that he has adduced justifies the assertion
that he has failed to point out a single inconsistency
between Dan. v. and the monuments. Now is it conceivable that a nameless Jew of a later age, whom the
critics, in order to make out their case, are obliged to
charge with gross ignorance of some very conspicuous
facts of the intervening history, is the author of a narrative detailing particulars respecting the last day of the
Babylonish empire, which have escaped the notice of
all ancient writers, but are signally confirmed by native
and contemporary inscriptions brought to light within
the last few years, in which he states that there was a Belshazzar; that he was in Babylon and in high authority
at the time of its final surrender; that he was descended
from Nebuchadnezzar (in spite of the fact that his
father was a usurper and not of royal blood); that the
queen is distinguished (ver. 10) from the wives of Belshazzar (ver. 3); that she was living at the fall of the
city (if Schrader reads correctly); that she was familiar
with facts in the reign of Nebuchadnezzar, of which Belshazzar appears to have been ignorant; that she was a
superior person, calculated to win universal respect, as
shown by her calm and dignified demeanor in the midst
of a terror-stricken assemblage. In the statement of
these minute circumstances, otherwise unknown, there
is abundant opportunity for anyone to trip who was
not perfectly familiar with the facts with which he was
dealing. And yet the writer of this book has threaded
his way through them all without being convicted of a
single blunder. And it may be added that the inscription of Cyrus, which declares that his army entered
Babylon without opposition, has falsified the statements
of other historians on the subject, but Daniel remains
uncontradicted. He speaks of no siege and no strata-
gem to gain admission to the walls. He simply says

that Belshazzar was slain, and that the kingdom was transferred to the Medes and Persians. Here is another chance for a blunder. Nabuna'id survived the fall of Babylon, but, if Hagen reads correctly, there is monumental evidence that Belshazzar did not. Can we fail to see in all this the hand of one present at the scene, and who knows whereof he affirms?

f. " Darius, son of Ahasuerus—elsewhere the Hebrew form of *Xerxes*—a *Mede,* after the death of Belshazzar, is ' made king over the realm of the Chaldeans' (v. 31, vi. 1 ff., ix. 1, xi. 1). There seems to be no room for such a ruler. According to all other authorities, Cyrus is the immediate successor of Nabu-nahid, and the ruler of the entire Persian empire."

But Sargon and Belshazzar admonish us not to be too hasty in imagining that the explicit statement of a sacred writer is in every case outweighed by the silence of other historians. Perhaps Darius the Mede may be the Cyaxares [1] of Xenophon, or he may be some noble of Median birth, to whom Cyrus found it convenient to commit the government of Babylon for a brief term. We can afford, in this instance, to wait for further light. The inscription of Cyrus records his entry into the city and the submission of its inhabitants and of the surrounding region, but beyond the appointment of some subordinate officials says nothing of the arrangements for its government. So far then from there being " no room for such a ruler," the way is entirely open for any ruler whom Cyrus might see fit to place in authority over this conquered kingdom. Dr. Driver gratuitously utters the groundless suspicion that the writer has here confused distinct persons, and that Darius the Mede is " a reflection into the past of Darius Hystaspes," though in his first edition he acknowledged that "the circum-

[1] So Josephus, Ant., x. 11, 4.

stances are not, perhaps, such as to be absolutely inconsistent with either the existence or the office of Darius the Mede; and a cautious criticism will not build too much on the silence of the inscriptions, where many certainly remain yet to be brought to light."

g. "In ix. 2 it is stated that Daniel 'understood by *the books*' the number of years for which, according to Jeremiah, Jerusalem should lie waste. The expression used implies that the prophecies of Jeremiah formed part of a *collection* of sacred books which, nevertheless, it may safely be affirmed, was not formed in 536 B.C."

It is difficult to see with what propriety such an affirmation can be made, or what there was to prevent Daniel from having in his possession the inspired books, so far as they had then been written, and among them the prophecies of Jeremiah.

h. "Other indications adduced to show that the book is not the work of a contemporary are such as the following: The improbability that Daniel, a strict Jew, should have suffered himself to be initiated into the class of Chaldean 'wise men,' or should have been admitted by the wise men themselves (ch. i.; cf. ii. 13); Nebuchadnezzar's seven years' insanity (lycanthropy), with his edict respecting it; the absolute terms in which both he and Darius (iv. 1–3, 34–37, vi. 25–27), while retaining, so far as appears, their idolatry, recognize the supremacy of the God of Daniel, and command homage to be done to Him."

It is surely not worth while to waste time and space in giving a serious answer to frivolous objections of this nature, which might be multiplied to any extent. It is sufficient to quote Dr. Driver's own words in regard to them: "The circumstances alleged will appear improbable or not improbable, according as the critic, upon independent grounds, has satisfied himself that the book is the work of a later author or written by Daniel himself."

In the opinion of Dr. Driver, the arguments above recited " tend to show that this book reflects the traditions and historical impressions of an age considerably later than that of Daniel himself." There seems to be nothing to justify this conclusion. On the contrary, the accuracy of its statements, even in minute particulars, wherever it is possible to test them by comparison with other trustworthy sources, its acquaintance with facts mentioned by no other historian, but recently confirmed by contemporary monuments, and its general correspondence with all that is known of the situation assumed, show a familiarity on the part of the writer with the scenes described such as could not be expected in a Jew residing in Palestine two or more centuries later, but which agrees exactly with the claim which it makes for itself of being the work of Daniel, a high official in the court of Babylon.

In regard to the language of the Book of Daniel, Dr. Driver says : " The *Persian* words presuppose a period after the Persian empire had been well established ; the Greek words *demand*, the Hebrew *supports*, and the Aramaic *permits*, a date *after the conquest of Palestine by Alexander the Great*, B.C. 332."

This is a sweeping conclusion from very slender and precarious premises. Like Persian words occur in Ezra, Nehemiah, Esther, and Chronicles. Why might they not be used also by Daniel, who was brought into immediate contact with Persian monarchs and officers ? And who can assure us that Arian words, which can now be best explained from the Persian, had not wandered into the popular speech of the great metropolis of Babylon before its conquest by Cyrus, even though they have not yet been found in the inscriptions? The Greek words, of which earlier critics had scraped together a formidable list, have now been reduced to three names of musical instruments. One of these is a Homeric word, which, Dr. Driver admits, might have travelled into the East. And though the other two do not chance to appear in this sense in Greek literature until a later time, this does not disprove their existence in ordinary speech, nor the possibility of their being carried to Babylon. Delitzsch[1] says on this subject, "Why should not three Greek instruments have been known in Babylon, the 'city of merchants,' as Ezekiel calls it, in the pre-seleucid period? A recent philologist[2] says, without having the Book of Daniel in mind, and, therefore, quite unbiassed in his judgment: 'The extended trade of the Greek colonies must not seldom have brought Greek merchants into Assyrian countries. They even penetrated beyond the Volga far into the inhospitable steppes of Russia on the Don. But the intercourse with the Assyrian provinces of Asia Minor must have been most considerable. That Greeks came as merchants even to Assyria itself is and must remain only a supposition, but it is certain that Greek soldiers accompanied Esarhaddon in his expeditions through Asia, and that, generally speaking, the West took part to a greater extent in the revolutions of the East than one would believe is shown by the fragment of a poetical letter of Alcæus to his brother Antimenides, who had won glory and stipend under the standard of Nebuchadnezzar.' Accordingly, acquaintance with three Greek instruments would not be surprising nor inexplicable even in Nineveh, not to say in Babylon under the later Chaldean dominion."

Dr. Driver alleges that "the Aramaic of Daniel,

---

[1] Herzog Encyk., 1st edition, III., p. 274.
[2] John Brandis, Allgem. Monatsschrift, 1854, 2.

(which is all but identical with that of Ezra) is a *Western* Aramaic dialect, of the type spoken in and about *Palestine.*" Delitzsch [1] was of a different opinion : "Affinity with the Palestine Aramaic is lacking entirely; it is with the Aramaic of the Book of Ezra the oldest East Aramaic monument preserved to us." And the interchange of Hebrew and Aramean is precisely similar to that in Ezra. The Hebrew of the book has fewer anomalies than that of Ezekiel, and corresponds with that of Chronicles, Ezra, and Nehemiah. The critics arbitrarily assign these books to the close of the Persian or beginning of the Greek period, and undertake to support this position by the unwarranted assertion that the common character of their language is indicative of this late date; but this is a figment used to bolster up a foregone critical conclusion. These books belong to the period of Ezra and Nehemiah, and determine the language of their time. And the agreement of Daniel with them in this respect points to a period not far removed from them. In the words of Delitzsch,[2] "In short, the total impression of the form of the language corresponds to the time of composition claimed by the Book of Daniel." And this is not discredited by the fact that Zechariah adhered somewhat more closely to the Hebrew of earlier books.

As the historical and linguistic objections are insufficient to disprove Daniel's authorship, it remains to be seen whether the dogmatic objections are any more decisive. If the atheistic or pantheistic position is taken, that miracles and predictive prophecy are impossible, and that doctrinal development can be no other than a purely natural growth, the question is settled; Daniel cannot have been the author of the book. But to those

[1] Herzog-Plitt Encyk., III., p. 471.
[2] Herzog Encyk., III., p. 274.

who are theists, and who believe that God has made a
revelation to men, authenticated by immediate mani-
festations of His presence and power, the advanced
teachings of this book, the miracles which it records,
and the clear prevision of the future here displayed,
cannot be accepted as proofs that it is not what it claims
to be, what it has traditionally been believed to be,
and what, according to our Lord's teaching, it is.

Dr. Driver infers that this book belongs to "a later
age than that of the exile," because "the doctrines of
the Messiah, of angels, of the resurrection, and of a
judgment on the world, are taught with greater distinctness, and in a more developed form, than elsewhere in
the Old Testament." But it is difficult to see why fresh
revelations on these subjects might not be made to
Daniel, as well as to one in the period of the Maccabees.
The inspired writer of the Epistle to the Hebrews believed that there were those who, through faith, had
"stopped the mouths of lions, and quenched the vio-
lence of fire"; why may we not believe it, too?

But it is chiefly to the predictions that Dr. Driver
objects:

1. "That the revelations respecting Antiochus Epiphanes should be given to Daniel, in *Babylon*, nearly
four centuries previously."

2. "The minuteness of the predictions, embracing
even special events in the distant future."

3. "While down to the period of Antiochus' persecution the *actual* events are described with surprising distinctness, after this point *the distinctness ceases:* the
prophecy either breaks off altogether, or merges in an
ideal representation of the Messianic future."

But (1) the Bible contains numerous predictions of
the remote future, and these often relating to specific
events, which are exactly stated or more or less minutely

described. It was revealed to Abraham that a great
nation should descend from him (Gen. xii. 2), which
should possess the land of Canaan (ver. 7), but should
first be in bondage in a foreign land four hundred years,
on which judgments should be inflicted, and then they
should come out with great substance (xv. 13, 14). To
Isaac, that Esau's descendants should serve Jacob, but
should ultimately throw off his yoke (xxvii. 40). To
Jacob, many particulars respecting the settlement of the
tribes in Canaan, including the sceptre in Judah (ch.
xlix.). To Balaam, the sceptre that should rise out of
Israel and smite surrounding lands, the triumphs of
Assyria, and its overthrow (Num. xxiv.). To Moses,
that Israel should suffer from distant invaders, and be
carried into exile (Deut. xxviii.). To Isaiah, at the very
outset of his ministry, the desolation and captivity of
Judah (v. 13, 26–30, vi. 11, 12); at the beginning of the
reign of Ahaz, the Assyrian invasion and its inglorious
issue (vii. 17 ff., viii. 7–10), which he continued to reiter-
ate until Sennacherib's disastrous overthrow; when
Hezekiah vaingloriously displayed his treasures to messengers from Babylon, that these should be carried
thither into captivity (xxxix. 6, 7), but that Babylon
itself should fall and be reduced to utter desolation
(chs. xiii., xiv.), and Judah's exiles be released by Cyrus
(xliv. 26, 28). To Micah, that Zion should be ploughed
as a field, and its people exiled to Babylon, and there
delivered (iii. 12, iv. 10). To Jeremiah, the precise du-
ration of the captivity (xxv. 11, 12), the utter desolation
of Edom (xlix. 17), and the fall of Babylon (chs. li., lii.).
To Zechariah, the victory of Zion over the Grecian army
of Antiochus Epiphanes (ix. 13). If there is any truth
in the representations of Scripture on this subject, there
have been numberless predictions of specific events in
the distant future. Those who deny the possibility of

predictive prophecy, act consistently in unsparingly applying the last resource of the critics, and sweeping away every vestige of clear and remote predictions by summarily setting aside their genuineness, if they cannot rid themselves of them in any other way.   But it is surely very inconsistent in those who admit the reality of a divinely inspired foresight of the future, to prescribe in advance the limits and bounds within which alone this may be exercised, and to refuse to acknowledge the genuineness of any prophecy which exceeds the restrictions that they have arbitrarily imposed upon it.

(2.) The specific predictions of Daniel do not terminate with Antiochus Epiphanes.   The four empires of chs. ii. and vii. are the Babylonian, Medo-Persian, Greek, and Roman.   The attempts to find four empires answering to these visions without including the Roman are manifest evasions.   The Medo-Persian cannot be divided into two.   The Medes and Persians were under one sovereignty, and so are uniformly combined in the Book of Daniel (v. 28, vi. 8, 12, 15, viii. 20), in Esther (i. 3, 14, 18, 19), and repeatedly in the Behistun inscription of Darius Hystaspes.   Besides, the Persian cannot be the third of Daniel's empires, since it does not correspond with the third beast of his vision, which had four heads (vii. 6), indicating its fourfold division, which was true of the Greek empire (viii. 8, 22), but not of the Persian.   Nor can the Greek empire be divided by counting the empire of Alexander the third, and that of his successors, and particularly the Syrian branch, from which Antiochus Epiphanes sprang, the fourth.   For the third beast with its four heads must symbolize an empire broken into four parts, and must, therefore, include the empire of Alexander's successors along with that of Alexander himself.   The fourth empire is represented as stronger and more terrible than any that had preceded it, but it is expressly said that the power of Alexander's successors would not equal his own (viii. 22, xi. 4). And no satisfactory account can be given of the ten horns or ten kingdoms to arise out of the fourth beast, if this be the empire of Alexander's successors.

The only plausible argument in favor of making the fourth beast represent the Greek empire is the assumed identity of the little horn in vii. 8, 24, 25, and that in viii. 9–12, 23–25, which are described in somewhat similar terms. That in ch. viii. is undoubtedly Antiochus Epiphanes; but that in ch. vii. is his counterpart, who was to arise at a much later time, the Antichrist of the New Testament (2 Thes. ii. 3, 4, 8–10; 1 John, ii. 18; Rev. xiii. 5–7).

The prophecy of the seventy weeks (ix. 24–27) was fulfilled in the ministry and vicarious death of Jesus Christ at the predicted time, and in the destruction of Jerusalem by the Romans (cf. Matt. xxiv. 15, 16). The attempt to apply this to Antiochus Epiphanes both requires a wresting of its terms, and assumes a strange ignorance of chronology on the part of the supposed Maccabean writer.

(3.) It is quite in accordance with the analogy of prophecy, when Daniel clearly predicts the struggle of the Maccabees against Antiochus, and blends with the deliverances of that period the blessings of Messiah's reign. Messiah is ordinarily the background of every prophetic picture. It is so with Isaiah, Jeremiah, and the prophets generally. Zechariah predicts the contest with the Syro-Macedonian empire, and then, precisely as Daniel does, hurries away from it to the coming of Christ (ix. 8, 9; cf. ver. 13). Nevertheless the prediction that the Greek empire would be followed by the Roman, shows that Daniel did not expect the resurrection and final judgment to follow immediately after the deliverance from the persecutions of Antiochus, and thus corrects the false inferences drawn from the transition in xii. 1, 2. Moreover, if the Book of Daniel were a spurious production, first written and published B.C. 165, and contained the extravagant and fanatical expectations which have been imputed to it respecting the miraculous death of Antiochus in Palestine, to be followed at once by the coming of the Messiah and the resurrection — expectations which were falsified by the event within two years—must it not have been discredited at once ? How could it ever have gained credit as the genuine work of a true prophet of God, and even have been attributed to one who lived nearly four centuries before, though now heard of for the first time? And especially how could it have gained such speedy and acknowledged influence as to have been at once inserted in the sacred canon, and that the Book of Maccabees, in recording the history of these times, adopts its very language and borrows its forms of expression ? Not to add that there is strong reason to believe that the Septuagint version of the Book of Daniel was in existence before the date assigned by the critics for its composition.

(4.) The attempts which have been made to compromise by accepting the critical conclusions adverse to the genuineness of the Book of Daniel, and at the same time holding to its inspired character as a product of divine revelation, are as futile here as in regard to other books of the Old Testament which have been similarly treated. They only result in retaining all the difficulties which have been thought to encumber the traditional belief as to its authorship, and in introducing others of a far more formidable character.

Dr. Driver thinks that the author was "a prophet living in the time of the trouble itself," who wrote "not *after* the persecutions were ended, but at *their begin-*

ning," and "thus uttered genuine predictions." "Genuine predictions," as distinguished from mere lucky conjectures or shrewd calculations from existing causes, which involve a real provision of what lay beyond the reach of the human faculties, are the essence of the difficulty to those who would explain everything from natural causes. This is not relieved by reducing their number, or by shortening the time prior to their fulfilment. And "the distinctness of the prophecy merging in an ideal representation of the Messianic future," to which Dr. Driver objects, remains equally upon his own view of the case. But if the author of the book is a true prophet, and utters "genuine prophecies," why does he not come forward in his real character, and utter them in his own name as a messenger sent from God, as every other prophet does, and as an honest man must do, instead of falsely ascribing to a prophet of a former age what he never uttered?

Dr. Driver tells us, further, that "the book rests upon a *traditional basis.* Daniel, it cannot be doubted, was a historical person, one of the Jewish exiles in Babylon who, with his three companions, was noted for his stanch adherence to the principles of his religion, who attained a position of influence at the court of Babylon, who interpreted Nebuchadnezzar's dreams, and foretold as a seer something of the future fate of the Chaldean and Persian empires. Perhaps written materials were at the disposal of the author. . . . The narratives in chs. i.–vi. are thus adapted to supply motives for the encouragement, and models for the imitation, of those suffering under the persecution of Antiochus. In chs. vii.–xii. definiteness and distinctness are given to Daniel's visions of the future." We must confess that our confidence in the truth of the facts above recited rests upon the testimony of Daniel himself, rather than the amiable assurance given by Dr. Driver, who has found them "mingled with much that is unhistorical." And, after all, he gives no hint whether the miraculous interferences on behalf of God's servants in chs. i.–vi. are facts or fictions. If the former, why might not Daniel have recorded them? If the latter, they would be fallacious grounds of "encouragement" or "imitation." And so far as "definiteness and distinctness are given to Daniel's visions of the future" in chs. vii.–xii. by the author of the book in its present form, he has falsified them. He has attributed to Daniel definite and distinct predictions, which in fact he did not make. Such a defence, involving moral obliquity, is more to be deprecated than open assault.

The existence of Maccabean Psalms is a vexed question, in regard to which there is the widest possible diversity of opinion among critics. Justus Olshausen, von Lengerke, Reuss, and Cheyne find a large number, scattered through every part of the Book of Psalms, which they attribute to this period. According to Hitzig, Pss. i., ii., lxxiii.–cl. are Maccabean. Others of more moderate views, like Delitzsch and Perowne, are content with referring Pss. xliv., lxxiv., lxxix. to that date. Robertson Smith, who had included these three Psalms among those of Maccabean origin in the first edition of his "Old Testament in the Jewish Church," no longer regarded them as such in his second edition, but assigns Pss. cxviii., cxlix., and a few others in the latter part of the collection to the early years of Maccabee sovereignty. On the other hand, such critics as Gesenius, Maurer, De Wette, Bleek, Ewald, Hengstenberg, Hävernick, Keil, Dillmann, and many others deny that any Psalms belong to the Maccabean period, and insist that those which have been so referred with any plausibility find their true explanation in the ravages of the Chaldeans when

Jerusalem was destroyed by Nebuchadnezzar, or the troubles succeeding the return from the exile. The fact is, as Dr. Driver says, p. 388, " The grounds upon which specific dates can be assigned to individual Psalms are often exceedingly slender." The criteria urged for the reference of particular Psalms to the Maccabean period are of that general and indefinite sort that will apply equally well, and often much better, to other and earlier times of oppression and trial.

We have now examined with some care the reasons adduced to show that Chronicles, Ezra, Nehemiah, Ecclesiastes, Esther, and Daniel belong to a later date than the reign of Artaxerxes Longimanus, and have found them unsatisfactory. The divergence among critics in respect to Maccabean Psalms is such, and the grounds urged in their favor are so vague and inconclusive, that their existence must be considered very problematical. The statement of the historian Josephus that no addition was made to the canon after the reign of Artaxerxes Longimanus, and the current belief of the nation of the Jews that Malachi was the last of the prophets, and that after him the Holy Spirit departed from Israel, thus remain uncontradicted, except by critical theories which rest on no solid foundation.

VI

THE THREEFOLD DIVISION OF THE CANON

THE first notice that we have of the canon of the Old Testament after its completion is in the prologue to the Book of Ecclesiasticus. The writer, by whom this work of his grandfather, Jesus the son of Sirach, was translated into Greek, speaks of the sacred books as "the law, and the prophets, and the others that followed after them"; then of his grandfather giving himself largely to the reading of "the law and the prophets and the other books of the fathers"; and still further, by way of apology for the inferiority of his translation to the original work, that this is the case even with "the law and the prophets and the rest of the books," as rendered from the Hebrew into another tongue. The proximate date of this prologue, as appears from a statement contained in it, is the thirty-eighth year of Ptolemy Euergetes, king of Egypt. As the first of that name did not reign so long, this must be Ptolemy Euergetes II., commonly called Physcon, whose thirty-eighth year would correspond with B.C. 130. Accordingly at that time, and also in the time of the writer's grandfather, fifty or more years earlier, the sacred books formed a definite and well-known collection, arranged in three divisions, severally denominated "the law and the prophets and the other books," or "the rest of the books." This is the same division that existed ever afterward, and is now found in the Hebrew Bible. It has been alleged that the third division was then only in the process of formation, and did not yet contain all the books which subsequently belonged to it.   But the terms in which it is described are as definite and explicit as those applied to the other two divisions.   There is no more reason to regard it as open to later additions than there is in the case of the law and the prophets.   That it does not receive an equally descriptive designation is due to the somewhat miscellaneous character of its contents.   The designations here used correspond precisely to those of later times—law, prophets, and k'thubhim (writings) or hagiographa (sacred writings).

This division differs in form and in its determining principle from the fourfold division, adopted in all modern versions from the Greek Septuagint, into the law, the historical, the poetical, and the prophetical books, based upon the distinctive character of these different classes of sacred writings.

The threefold division of the Hebrew canon rests, not upon the nature of the contents of the several books, but upon the personality of the writers.   And here the distinction lies not in the various grade of their inspiration, as was maintained by Maimonides and the rabbins of the Middle Ages, who held that the law stood first, because Moses, its author, spake with God face to face ; that the prophets, who came next, were inspired by the Spirit of prophecy, while the writers of the k'thubhim had a lower grade of inspiration, viz.: that of the Holy Spirit.   The real ground of the division is the official status of the sacred writers.   Moses, as the great legislator and founder of the Old Testament dispensation, occupied a unique position, and his books appropriately stand by themselves in the first place.

Then follow in the second place the prophets, a distinct order of men, universally recognized as such, the immediate messengers of God to the people to declare his will and purposes to them for their guidance, instruction, and admonition. Their writings are of two kinds, historical and prophetical. In the former they trace the hand of God in his past dealings ; in the latter they deliver the messages with which they have been charged. Their historical writings are called the former prophets, and their prophetical writings the latter prophets, from the order in which they stand in the canon.

Finally, the third division comprises the writings of inspired men, who were not prophets in the technical and official sense. David was gifted with divine inspiration, and the Psalms composed by him contain Messianic predictions ; but he held the office of a king, not of a prophet. So with Solomon. Asaph and the sons of Korah were inspired singers, whose function was to lead the devotional worship of the temple ; they were not officially prophets. Consequently the writings of David, Solomon, Asaph and the sons of Korah properly stand not among those of the prophets, but with the k'thubhim.

The principle upon which the classification is made is thus a clear and obvious one ; the three divisions contain respectively the writings of Moses, of the prophets, and of inspired men not prophets.

Dillmann [1] says "It is very easily understood why the prophets are separated from the law, and again the books of the poets from the prophets ; also why the historical books are put together with the books of the prophets in one division. . . . From these are rightly distinguished the books of the men of God, who without having the official and public position of the prophets are yet filled with the spirit of wisdom and knowledge, and impelled by the forces of a divine life

[1] Jahrb. f. D. Theol., III., p. 425.

within them, have left the Church written monuments of their inner spiritual life. So far the division is quite clear and transparent, and likewise of the kind that it could without scruple be derived from one primal and original collector of these three parts." If, then, the three divisions of the canon had contained severally the law, the prophets (including both the historical and the prophetical books), and the books of the poets, they might, according to Dillmann, have been referred to a single collector, who arranged them thus at one time. He is, however, disturbed by the fact that the third division is not restricted to poetical books. Hence he goes on to say, "But besides the books of the poets there are also found in the third portion of the canon some historical books, Chronicles with Ezra (including Nehemiah) and Esther, and a prophetical book, Daniel; books, therefore, which according to the above principle of division one would expect to be in the second portion, or in the canon of the prophets."

Moses Stuart claims that as originally arranged the third division of the canon merely contained the poetical books.[1] He appeals in proof to the son of Sirach, who in his praise of famous men speaks of prophecies, Ecclus. xliv. 3, poems, ver. 5, and the law of Moses (xlv. 5); to Philo,[2] who says of the Therapeutæ that "they receive only the laws, and the oracles uttered by the prophets, and the hymns and other books by which knowledge and piety are augmented and perfected," the "other books" being immediately after described as "the writings of ancient men, the leaders of their sect"; to Luke, xxiv. 44 "the law of Moses and the prophets and the Psalms," Psalms being here supposed to

[1] Old Testament Canon, pp. 248 ff., 292.
[2] De Vita Contemplativa; this treatise is now believed not to be by Philo, but of later date.

be used in a wide sense to embrace all the poetical books ; to Josephus, who after speaking of the first and second divisions of the canon describes the third by saying, " the other four books contain hymns to God and maxims of life for men " ; and to the catalogues of the early Christian fathers, which in enumerating the books of Scripture put all the poetical books together. Whereupon he concludes "that the son of Sirach, Philo, the New Testament, Josephus, and all the earlier Christian writers down to the middle of the fourth century testify in favor of an arrangement of the Hebrew Scriptures, which classed four books together that are of like composition and matter in some important respects, and regards only these as belonging to the Hagiographa. All that differs from this is later." [1]

But the Christian catalogues are more or less governed by the fourfold classification of the Septuagint, and shed no light upon the triple division of the Hebrew canon. Josephus classifies the books for a purpose of his own without designing to give the arrangement in the canon. In Luke, xxiv. 44 "Psalms " simply means the book so called, and is not intended to be descriptive of a particular division of the canon. And the passages cited from Ecclesiasticus and that relating to the Therapeutæ simply speak of hymns and poems among the sacred books without implying anything as to the order of their arrangement in the collection.

The real explanation of the whole matter is, as above stated, that in constituting the Hebrew canon the books were not classified by the nature of their contents, nor as poetry and prose, but by the official status of their writers. The books of Moses stand in the first division,

---

[1] The same position substantially was taken previously by Storr in Paulus's Neues Repertorium, II , pp. 226 ff., as mentioned by Dillmann.

those of prophets in the second, those of inspired men not prophets in the third.

The books of Ezra and Nehemiah contain histories of an important period in the life of the chosen people, but they were written by the eminent men whose names they bear. Ezra was a scribe, Nehemiah was a governor, but neither of them were prophets. Their books consequently could not be classed with the other historical books, which were written by prophets, but with the books of inspired men who were not prophets. The same is the case with Chronicles. Though the history which it contains is closely related with that found in Samuel and Kings, the authorship was different. Samuel and Kings were, or were believed to be, the work of prophets, and are, therefore, classed as books of prophets. Chronicles, it is commonly believed, is from the same pen as the Book of Ezra, by an inspired man, but not by a prophet, and its proper place is accordingly in the third division.

The Book of Daniel appears at first sight to create some difficulty, and to be at variance with the principle of classification, which has determined the disposition of books in the sacred canon. Daniel is distinctly called a prophet in the New Testament (Matt. xxiv. 15; Mark xiii. 14), prophetic visions were granted to him, and his book contains some of the most remarkable predictions in the Bible. Why then is not this book classed with the books of the prophets in the second division of the canon, instead of being ranked with those of inspired men not prophets in the third and last division?[1] The reason is, because this is its

[1] Theodoret censures the Jews for having improperly removed Daniel from among the prophets, Bloch, Studien, p. 11. Ryle, p. 212, quotes Leusden, Philologus Hebræus, and John Smith, Discourse of Prophecy, as of the same mind in modern times.

proper place. This is not a departure from the principle previously announced, but a rigorous carrying out
of that principle. A distinction must here be made between the *donum propheticum* or the prophetic gift and
the *munus propheticum* or the prophetic office. Daniel
had the prophetic gift in a most extraordinary degree,
but he did not hold the prophetic office.[1] He did not
belong to the prophetic order like his fellow-captive and
contemporary Ezekiel, who dwelt among the exiles and
labored with them for their spiritual good. He had a
different office to perform on behalf of the people at the
court of Babylon, where he was ranked with the wise
men, and was advanced to a high political station.
Officially he was not a prophet, but occupied a lofty
position in the Babylonian and subsequently in the
Persian empire. He is called a prophet in the New
Testament in the same general sense in which that term
is applied to David (Acts ii. 29, 30).

Ryle[2] calls this explanation of the position of Daniel
in the canon "fanciful trifling" and "almost absurd in
its obvious inadequacy," without saying why he so regards it. Wildeboer[3] and Buhl[4] allege that "Amos
(vii. 12 ff.) overthrows the whole theory; for according to
it his book ought to stand among the K'thubhim."
Amos there says that he was no prophet, nor the son
of a prophet; but Jehovah took him as he followed the
flock and said unto him, Go, prophesy unto my people
Israel. This call of Jehovah surely made him a prophet,
though he was not one before.

Dillmann[5] objects: "Did Daniel then receive his rev-

---

[1] So Witsius, Hengstenberg, Hävernick, Keil, Oehler, Delitzsch,
and others.

[2] Canon of the Old Testament, pp. 122, 211 note.

[3] Canon of O. T., p. 18.   [4] Kanon und Text d. A. T., p. 37.

[5] Jahrb. f. D. Th. III., p. 427.

elations for himself alone, and not rather for the Church, even though that of the future? Was not the duty and the office of publication in writing likewise obligatory upon him? And is then the office of publication in writing so entirely different from that by oral delivery? Is not this rather a wholly external distinction, which does not touch the essence of the matter?" But this is entirely aside from the question at issue. Whether it does or does not agree with modern notions to make this distinction is of small consequence. As Dillmann himself says in discussing another aspect of this question, "The Old Testament canon was fixed by the Jewish Church . . . so that the only thing of consequence is, what idea did the Jewish Church connect with this division?" Now it is unquestionable that while the term "prophet" was frequently used in a broad and general sense, and applied to any who were divinely inspired, the Jews did recognize a distinct body of men as prophets in the strict, official sense, with prerogatives and functions peculiarly their own. And it was the writings of this class of men, as distinguished from all others, who, though truly inspired, were not intrusted with these functions, that were placed in the second division of the canon. The Book of Daniel makes revelations of great importance to his own as well as future ages, but does not occupy itself with rebukes of sin or inculcations of duty, as is usual in the prophets, or as might be expected if he were directly charged with laboring for their spiritual welfare.

Driver (p. 509) calls attention to this peculiarity of the book : "It is remarkable also," he says, "that Daniel —so unlike the prophets generally—should display no interest in the welfare or prospects of his contemporaries." From this he draws the erroneous conclusion that the book does not belong to the period when it claims to have been written. It did serve an important purpose for that time in letting the people know that the glories of the Messianic period were not to follow immediately upon the return from the exile, and giving them an intimation of what lay still before them prior to its arrival. But the marked difference between this book and those of the prophets generally is due to the fact that the function assigned to Daniel differed from that of the prophets.

The Book of Lamentations is in the present arrangement of the Hebrew Bible put in the Hagiographa, but there is good reason to believe that it originally stood in the second division of the canon. We learn from the testimony of Origen, Jerome, and other early writers that Ruth and Lamentations were sometimes reckoned as separate books, and sometimes regarded simply as appendices to other books, Ruth being attached to Judges, and Lamentations to Jeremiah. The books were so combined that when Ruth and Lamentations were counted as separate books, the whole number was made out to be twenty-four, the number of letters in the Greek alphabet; and when they were left uncounted, being regarded as included in other books, the whole number was twenty-two, the number of letters in the Hebrew alphabet.[1] It is natural to suppose that the latter mode of reckoning was the primitive one

[1] Cosin (Scholastical History of the Canon, p. 12, note i.) quotes from Sixtus Senensis : " As with the Hebrews there are 22 letters, in which all that can be said and written are comprehended, so there are 22 books in which are contained all that can be known and uttered of divine things."   Jerome expresses himself similarly in his Prologus Galeatus : " As there are 22 elements by which we write in Hebrew all that we speak, and in them the human voice is primarily embraced, so there are reckoned 22 books in which as in letters and rudiments the tender infancy of the just man is instructed in the doctrine of God."

among the Jews; and this is the common opinion of scholars. And if this be so, the original place of the Lamentations of Jeremiah is where we should expect to find it, in the second division of the canon, among the productions of the prophets.

To this Strack[1] objects (1) that Ruth and Lamentations are not contained in the Targum of Jonathan on the Prophets, and consequently they could not have been in the second division of the canon when it was prepared; (2) that there is no trace in the tradition, whether of Palestinian or Babylonish Jews, of Ruth having ever been attached to Judges or Lamentations to Jeremiah; (3) that according to the testimony of the Talmud (a Baraitha[2] in Berachoth) Psalms, Proverbs, and Job were called the three greater K'thubhim, and the Song of Solomon, Ecclesiastes, and Lamentations the three smaller K'thubhim; (4) that twenty-four as the number of the sacred books is suggested by 4 Esdras (E. V. 2 Esdras) xiv. 44–46, and is uniformly found in all Jewish tradition, so far as it is not influenced by the Alexandrians, there not being the slightest trace of the number twenty-two in either the Talmud or any Midrash.

[1] Herzog-Plitt Encyk., VII., pp. 433 ff.

[2] Baraitha means *outside ;* this term is applied to sections of the Talmud, which were not admitted to the Mishnah, though attributed to the Tannaim (*i.e.* Repeaters) or Jewish doctors from the time of the destruction of Jerusalem by Titus down to and including R. Judah the Holy, who reduced the Mishnah (*i.e.* Repetition, viz., of the Oral Law traditionally preserved) to writing in its present form about the end of the second century A.D. The Baraithas are collectively called 'hosaphtah, *addition.* These, with the Mishnah, constitute the text of 'he Talmud, the comments upon which are called Gemara, *supplement,* and make up the remainder of that storehouse of Jewish traditions. The Gemara is in two forms, that of the Jerusalem Talmud, dating from about A.D. 425, and that of the Babylonish Talmud, about A.D. 500, and is the work of the doctors after the closing of the Mishnah, who are called Amoraim *Expounders.*

Strack's attempt to explain how the number twenty-two came into vogue in Alexandria does not seem to be successful. He thinks that the books of the Hebrew canon were there counted in the order in which they appear in the Septuagint translation, Ruth being next to Judges, and Lamentations to Jeremiah; these small books were hence considered as parts of the larger ones, and so the total was made twenty-two. But while in the Hebrew, Samuel, Kings, and Chronicles are each regarded as constituting one book, in the LXX. each of them is reckoned as two books; and Ezra and Nehemiah form together one book in Hebrew, but each is counted separately in the LXX.; so that the total would be spoiled. Septuagint influence cannot, therefore, account for the facts.

It appears to be much simpler to trace the number twenty-two to the current Jewish tradition attested by the Talmud (a Baraitha in Baba Bathra), that Ruth was written by the author of Judges, and Lamentations by Jeremiah. They might thus be readily attached to the books which were thought to have proceeded from the same pen. That this was the case in Palestine as well as Alexandria is evidenced by Josephus, Melito, and Jerome on the one hand, and by Origen on the other.

Fürst[1] gives the following account of the matter: "Besides this division [*i.e.*, into twenty-four books], which was sanctioned in Talmudic Judaism, a division into twenty-two books, parallel to the twenty-two letters of the alphabet, was in use in Palestine and Alexandria. . . . The division into twenty-four seems to have arisen in Babylonia, and as in all matters of Judaism, only that which was in use in the Babylonish schools established itself among the Jews."

[1] Der Kanon des Alten Testaments nach der Ueberlieferungen in Talmud und Midrasch, p. 4.

Bloch[1] truly says: "Without Ruth the historical part of the canon of the prophets would be incomplete and defective. It lacks the genealogy of the most powerful race of kings, with whose fortunes also the changeful past of the people and its glorious future, so eagerly and surely expected, was intimately interwoven—that of the house of Jesse. Ewald's assertion that such a genealogy had been contained in the Book of Samuel, and was only omitted in closing the canon of the prophets on account of Ruth iv., is so devoid of any scientific and tenable basis that we may properly decline to enter more particularly upon it, and the more as this assertion has as its presupposition the reception of Ruth into the canon of the prophets. . . . Its transfer to the Hagiographa did not take place until the Talmudic period, and then only for liturgical reasons."

Wildeboer (p. 141) holds that, in the first instance, "Ruth was probably generally placed after Judges and Lamentations after Jeremiah"; and that this arrangement was perpetuated in many "copies of the Prophets, which were more likely to be in the possession of private individuals than copies of the Kethubhim." The "official theory" of the scribes, however, was at variance with this popular usage, and classed them with the K'thubhim.

Bleek[2] states, perhaps in too positive a form, the probable facts in the case: "Ruth and Lamentations had this position [i.e., after Judges and Jeremiah] even in Hebrew manuscripts in early times, and the Hebrew Jews subsequently, after the second century A.D., put them among the books of the third class with the other

---

[1] Studien zur Geschichte der Sammlung der althebräischen Literatur, p. 25.

[2] Einleitung in das Alte Testament, 1860, p. 35.

Megilloth with reference to their use in public worship." [1]

The three divisions of the canon, accordingly, contain no indication of their having been formed at widely separated periods. There is no imperfection in the classification which requires such an explanation. There are no books in the third division which ought properly to be in the second, and which must be assumed to have been placed where they are, because the second division was already closed, and could not be reopened for their reception. Such an assumption is too precarious and improbable to build a theory upon in any event. There is no very intelligible reason why the collection of the prophets should at any time be considered closed, except because there was no other book entitled to be included in it. If at any time a book should be discovered or produced, which rightfully belonged in that collection, the collection is thus shown to be incomplete without this book, and why should it not be placed there? If, for instance, the critical theory of the Book of Daniel were correct, and this book, though actually produced in the time of the Maccabees, was inserted in the canon because believed to be the genuine production of Daniel, the contemporary of Ezekiel, and the proper place for such a book from such an author was among the prophets, why was it not placed alongside of Ezekiel, as it is in the Septuagint, where the classification was upon a principle which required it? It is just because the Hebrew canon

---

[1] In German Hebrew MSS. and in ordinary Hebrew Bibles the five Megilloth follow each other in the order in which they are appointed to be read in the service of the Synagogue, viz.: the Song of Solomon at the Passover; Ruth at Pentecost; Lamentations at the fast of the ninth of the month Ab; Ecclesiastes at the feast of Tabernacles; Esther at Purim.

was accurately classified upon a principle of its own
that the book stands where it does, in the K'thubhim
and not among the prophets.   And the same is the case
with the other books, in which critics claim that this
principle has been violated.   It cannot be shown to
have been departed from in a single instance.   The
classification is such as bears the marks of a single
mind, and has been interfered with by no disturbing
cause.

VII

WHEN AND BY WHOM COLLECTED

THE authority of the books constituting the canon does not depend upon their being gathered together in a single volume, or being arranged in a particular way. Each book would have the same divine authority, whether circulating separately or combined with others of like character. It was of great importance, however, in order to guard the sacred books from the danger of being lost or overlooked, or from the intrusion of books not entitled to be so regarded, that they should be visibly sundered from all others by being brought together in one collection, sanctioned by general acceptance at a time when their claims could be properly scrutinized, and thus certified to future ages as the duly attested writings of men inspired of God, and prepared by them for the benefit of his people in all time to come.

When and by whom was this collection made? According to Elias Levita, a distinguished rabbi of the time of the Reformation, this was the work of Ezra and the Great Synagogue, a body of one hundred and twenty men, assembled to assist him in the conduct of public affairs.[1] This was repeated after him by several Lutheran and Reformed theologians, by whom it was regarded as an incontrovertible fact, based on an ancient and uniform tradition. The only passage, however, in early Jewish literature, which connects Ezra and the

---

[1] Strack (p. 416) points out that substantially the same view was previously held by David Kimchi.

Great Synagogue in any way with the formation of the canon is the following from the Talmudic treatise, Baba Bathra :

" Moses wrote his book, and the section about Balaam and Job ; Joshua wrote his book and eight verses in the law ; Samuel wrote his book and Judges and Ruth ; David wrote the Book of Psalms at the hands of the ancients, Adam the first, Melchizedek, Abraham, Moses, Heman, Jeduthun, Asaph and the three sons of Korah ; Jeremiah wrote his book and the Book of Kings and Lamentations ; Hezekiah and his associates wrote Isaiah, Proverbs, the Song of Songs and Ecclesiastes. The men of the Great Synagogue wrote Ezekiel, the Twelve [Minor Prophets], Daniel and the Book of Esther. Ezra wrote his book and the genealogies of Chronicles to his time."

This singular passage has been variously interpreted and variously estimated. The word "wrote" has been understood to mean "composed" as an author, "transcribed" what had been previously written, "reduced to writing" what had been orally delivered, or "inserted in the canon." Hävernick (p. 41) gives it throughout the last of these senses, which was invented by Bertholdt (pp. 81, 86), but is wholly supposititious. Herzfeld [1] finds the four different senses in different clauses of this paragraph.

The most satisfactory explanation of this passage is given by Marx [2] (Dalman), who finds in it the views of Jewish doctors of the second century A.D. respecting the origin of the books of the Old Testament which are mere fanciful conjectures and of no value whatever. Jeremiah is the only one of the latter prophets to whom writings are attributed, since he is repeatedly said to

---

[1] Geschichte, III., p. 94.

[2] Traditio Rabbinorum Veterrima, pp. 41 ff.

have written his prophecies by divine direction (xxx. 2, xxxvi. 2, 4, 28, 32, xlv. 1). As no similar statement is made in the case of the other prophets, the Book of Isaiah is ascribed to the associates of his contemporary Hezekiah ; the same who are said (Prov. xxv. 1) to have completed the Book of Proverbs, to which the Song of Solomon and Ecclesiastes are here added. Ezekiel, the Twelve, and Daniel, together with Esther are similarly attributed to the men of the Great Synagogue ; the idea probably being that these books were preserved orally, until by the authority and under the direction of these two bodies they were put in writing.

Fürst (p. 131) argues that the "associates of Hezekiah" or, as he denominates them, the "college of Hezekiah," in order to do what is here attributed to them, must have been a permanent body and continued in existence for 280 years, from B.C. 724 to 444. But the Jewish doctors had no such thought. They did not entertain the modern critical notions of the composite character of the Book of Isaiah, and Proverbs, Canticles and Ecclesiastes were believed by them to be Solomon's. It is no prolonged task, therefore, which is assigned to them. Fürst also maintains, what many others have likewise held, that the Great Synagogue was an organization which lasted for two centuries and a half, from B.C. 444 to 196. There is nothing in Jewish tradition to favor this opinion except the fact that Simon the Just is said to have been one of its members. But according to Jewish ideas the Great Synagogue did not last more than forty years, and did not extend beyond the time of Ezra. Their chronology makes Simon the Just a contemporary of Alexander the Great, and Alexander the immediate successor of Darius Hystaspes.

It is quite supposable that Ezra might have had a

body of men to aid him in regulating the affairs of the nation, but there seems to be no clear evidence that such a body ever existed. Kuenen[1] maintains with great plausibility that the only historical basis for it is the assembly of the people (Neh. viii.-x.), gathered to hear the law and pledge themselves to obey it, and that this was transformed by the Talmudic doctors into an authoritative council. Whether this is so or not, there is no reason for attributing the collection of the canon to the Men of the Great Synagogue.

According to the theory of modern critics the process of canonization began in a preliminary way, B.C. 621, when Josiah bound the people to obey the book of the law found in the temple (which they identify with Deuteronomy exclusively), and more effectively when Ezra, B.C. 444, engaged the returned exiles to yield compliance to all the requirements of the entire Pentateuch (Neh. viii.-x.). The Pentateuch, and that only, was thenceforward canonical. After a long interval the prophets were added to the canon, somewhere between B.C. 300 and 200, as the limits are fixed by Ryle (pp. 108, 109). Later still a third division of the canon was formed, containing the K'thubhim. Its commencement is dated by Ryle (p. 173), in the beginning of the era of the Maccabean ascendency, B.C. 160 to 140, and its final ratification about A.D. 90, although "all the books included in the third group of the canon had obtained some measure of recognition, either complete and undisputed, or partial and disputed" before the death of John Hyrcanus II., B.C. 105. Wildeboer (p. 146) brings down the time of the final decision as to the contents of the canon to A.D. 200.

But it is an entirely false conception that Deuter-

[1] Gesammelte Abhandlungen, no. 4, Ueber die Männer der Grossen Synagoge.

onomy was first made canonical by Josiah, and the Pentateuch by Ezra. The transactions referred to were
simply the solemn and formal recognition of a divine
authority inherent in these books from their first publication. And the exclusive mention of the law in these
public transactions does not prove that canonical and
divine authority was vested in it alone. The contrary
is explicitly declared by Deuteronomy itself (xviii. 18,
19), which ascribes to the prophets an authority like that
of Moses. The law and the prophets are joined together
(2 Kin. xvii. 13 ff.), as alike binding upon Judah and
Israel, who were both exiled from their land because
they did not obey them. Ezra, in the very passage recording the covenant engagement of the people to obey
the law, traces all the calamities that had befallen them
to their neglect of the law and their maltreatment of the
prophets (Neh. ix. 26 ff.). The Prophet Zechariah does
the same (i. 4, 6, vii. 7, 12). These passages leave no
doubt that the utterances of the prophets were believed
to have the same divine sanction as the statutes of the
law, and a like divine penalty followed the transgression
of the one as of the other.

It is not sufficient, therefore, to say with Wildeboer
(p. 119) that "before the exile writings of the prophets
were eagerly read by the devout," as well as "in and
after the exile"; if at the same time it is maintained
that these books were not then possessed of canonical
authority. The reason why they were prized by pious
people was because they accepted them as the word of
God communicated through his servants the prophets.
Dillmann's statement (p. 441) is much nearer the truth:
"We can scarcely doubt that the higher reverence,
which is due to the word of God, would be paid also to
the written discourses of a prophet by the believers
among his contemporaries, at least from the time that

he had by his work gained recognition as a prophet of God, or his words had been divinely confirmed by the issue. And here, if anywhere, it must come to pass that the canonical validity of a writing would be coincident with its first appearance."

This is precisely what took place. The books of the prophets were received as the word of God by those who put faith in their divine messages orally delivered. The suggestion that the number of believers was at times very small and rarely included the mass of the people, and that false prophets abounded in the later years of the kingdom, in consequence of which the influence of the true prophets declined in the popular estimation, does not alter the significance of the fact already adverted to. It is to the true worshippers of Jehovah that we are to look for the willing reception and faithful transmission of his word. The books of the prophets had, from the first, canonical authority among them, which is not invalidated by the disregard of the unbelieving multitude. And when the twofold sifting of the exile and of the return from captivity had occurred, and a people obedient to the word of the Lord had replaced the degenerate race that perished in the destruction of the city, there can be no question in what esteem the books of the prophets were held, their divine authority being confirmed, as it was, by the fulfilment of their predictions alike of desolation and of returning favor.

1. Why then did Ezra only bind the people to obey the law ?[1] Because the meeting was held, not to define the full extent of their obligations, but for a particular

---

[1] It is the law which is exclusively spoken of by 1 Maccabees as adhered to by the faithful and forsaken by the godless (i. 52, ii. 21, 26, 27, etc.). Yet no one imagines on this account that there were no other books in the canon when 1 Maccabees was written.

practical purpose, which was best met by directing their attention to the specific requirements of the law. The obligations assumed (Neh. x. 29 ff.) concern the removal of certain evils which had made their appearance in this infant community, viz., inter-marriage with aliens, disregard of the sabbath and inadequate provision for the temple worship. There were definite legal statutes bearing on these matters which covered the whole case. The more general and spiritual instructions of the prophets would not so precisely have answered the end in view.[1]

2. As the Samaritans possess the Pentateuch, but no other book of the Old Testament, it has been argued that nothing but the Pentateuch could have been canonical among the Jews at the time that it was obtained by the Samaritans. It is commonly supposed to have been taken to them by the renegade priest, who was expelled by Nehemiah (Neh. xiii. 28), and eagerly accepted by them to substantiate their claim of being kindred to the Jews (Ezra iv. 2); a claim, which would have been strengthened by accepting all the books that were then regarded as sacred. But the mutilated canon of the Samaritans had a similar origin with those of early heretical sects in the Christian Church. They accepted what suited their own peculiar views, and arbitrarily rejected all the rest. They had their temple on Mount Gerizim, and altered the text of Deut. xxvii. 4 to give it sanction, claiming that this was the place where men ought to worship. No book which spoke approvingly of worship at Shiloh or Jerusalem could be ac-

---

[1] This is recognized by Wildeboer (p. 119), though colored by a wrong idea of the design of this solemn covenant, when he traces the omission of the prophets in this sacred engagement "chiefly to the fact that they have not the same immediate importance for the establishment of Ezra's theocracy as the priestly law."

cepted by them. They were thus necessarily limited to the Pentateuch, irrespective of the extent of the Jewish canon at the time.

3. The Scripture lessons of the Synagogue were originally taken exclusively from the Pentateuch, which is divided into sections that are read in course on successive sabbaths; at a later time selections from the prophets were read along with the law (Luke iv. 16, 17, Acts xiii. 15, 27); but a like use is not made of the K'thubhim in the regular sabbath lessons. This has been urged as confirmatory of the critical hypothesis that the three divisions of the canon mark three successive stages in its formation. It is alleged that the Scripture reading was in the first instance confined to the law, because it alone was canonical. Afterward, when the prophets were admitted to the canon, lessons were taken from them likewise; and the selection was limited to the prophets, because the K'thubhim had not yet been made canonical.

This, however, is not the real explanation. Nor is it to be sought in an imagined difference in the sacredness and authority of the three portions of the canon. The idea of three successive grades of inspiration, and the comparison of the law to the holy of holies, of the prophets to the holy place, and the K'thubhim to the outer court, are figments of later times.[1]

As Jehovah's covenant relation with Israel rested upon the basis of the law, and was conditioned upon its faithful observance, it is natural that from the very first institution of synagogue worship it should have a place in the service. It would not be long, however, before the

[1] "Their equal sanctity and dignity was expressly maintained with great emphasis with particular reference to those heretics who did not regard the Prophets and Hagiographa as Thora or canonical." Fürst, Kanon, pp. 51, 69.

need would be felt of enforcing the lessons of the law by the teachings of the prophets. Their historical books record the experience of the people in former ages, showing the blessing that attended obedience and the penalty that followed transgression. Their books of prophecy insist upon adherence to the true worship of Jehovah, illustrate and expound the spiritual intent of the law, and hold up to view the final issue to which it tends. We are imperfectly informed as to the use made of the K'thubhim in the service of the Synagogue in early times. Their employment, to some extent at least, for this purpose, is suggested by the fact that a Targum on Job is spoken of which was of equal age with that of Jonathan on the prophets. In general, however, the books of the K'thubhim were less adapted for Synagogue use or were appropriated to special services. The psalms were sung in the temple (Ps. xcii. according to its title on the sabbath; and Pss. xxiv., xlviii., xciv., xciii. according to the LXX. were appointed for different days of the week). The five Megilloth were assigned to festival days. Selections from the Hagiographa, from Job, Ezra, Nehemiah, Chronicles, Daniel, Proverbs, etc., were read throughout the entire night before the day of atonement,[1] and in connection with the smaller Pentateuch sections on Mondays and Thursdays and at the vesper service on the sabbath.[2] The Synagogue lessons are readily accounted for, therefore, without resorting to the critical hypothesis.

4. The terms "the law" (John x. 34, xii. 34, xv. 25; 1 Cor. xiv. 21), or "the law and the prophets" (2 Macc. xv. 9; Matt. v. 17, vii. 12, xxii. 40; Luke xvi. 16, 29, 31; Acts xxviii. 23; Rom. iii. 21), are sometimes used to de-

[1] Bloch, Studien, p. 10; Fürst, Kanon, p. 52; Buhl, Kanon und Text, p. 15.

[2] Fürst, p. 82.

note the entire Old Testament. It is claimed that this is a reminiscence of the time when first "the law" and afterward "the law and the prophets" comprised the entire canon. But the simple reason of this usage is that all the Scriptures may, with propriety, be called "the law" since they constitute the revealed and authoritative will of God. And "the law and the prophets" may either be put for the entire Old Testament by synecdoche, a principal part standing for the whole, or the prophets may be used in a wide sense for all the writings of inspired men, as in Mat. xiii. 35 a Psalm of Asaph, Ps. lxxviii. 2, is quoted "as spoken by the prophet." [1] Cf. Heb. i. 1. Moses is also called a prophet (Hos. xii. 13), and an enactment of the law is attributed to the prophets (Ezra ix. 11, 12).

Accordingly, Bloch (pp. 8, 15) modifies the critical argument, and as the entire Scriptures may be called indifferently "law" or "prophets" or "sacred writings," he infers that these titles are not in themselves distinctive, and could not have been employed as designations of the three several portions of the canon, if this division had been made at any one time. It was only because "law" had acquired a technical sense by a long and exclusive application to the books of Moses, that subsequent additions to the canon could be called "prophets"; and this term was long applied to a definite number of books before it acquired its special sense, so that others subsequently introduced could distinctively be called "k'thubhim" or "sacred writings." But this form of the argument is no more valid than the other. Although these terms admit of a wider application, it is plain that "law" and "prophets" in their strict sense are properly

---

[1] In Jewish writings the Hagiographa are frequently referred to prophets in this wide sense, Herzfeld, Geschichte, III., pp. 98, 99; Bloch, Studien, p. 12; Buhl, Kanon und Text, p. 37.

descriptive of those portions of the canon to which they are applied, while K'thubhim, as a distinct title, naturally denotes those sacred writings which fall under neither of the above categories.

5. Some additional arguments in defence of the position that the prophets were not admitted to the canon until long after the public recognition of the law in the time of Ezra, are built upon unsound critical conclusions. Thus (1), it has been inferred from apparent discrepancies between Samuel and Kings, on the one hand, and Chronicles on the other, that the former could not yet have been regarded as canonical circ. 300 B.C., when it is alleged that Chronicles was written.[1] But the inference is futile for two reasons: Chronicles does not discredit Samuel and Kings, as is here assumed, nor does it belong to so late a date, as has been before shown. The differences referred to arise from the difference in the aim and scope of these histories respectively. Chronicles, which was probably written by Ezra, though referred by critics without reason to a century or more after his time, is largely occupied with matters connected with the ritual service, which was then being restored, but to which the earlier histories paid much less attention. These additional facts are drawn from other reliable authorities, and the seeming discrepancies can be satisfactorily explained.

(2.) The Book of Isaiah is, in the opinion of the critics, a composite production. A considerable portion of chs. i.–xxxv. is assigned to Isaiah, but interspersed with several sections of varying length, which are attributed to the later years of the Babylonish exile or shortly after it. Then follow four historical chapters, chs. xxxvi.–xxxix. ; and finally, chs. xl.–lxvi., which are al-

[1] Ryle, Canon, p. 108 ; König, Einleitung, p. 448.

leged to belong to near the close of the exile. Here
Ryle concludes (p. 104) that the compilation of chs.
i.–xxxix. took place a short time "before the period of
Nehemiah" (B.C. 444), but that chs. xl.–lxvi., though not
of so late a date as some of the preceding chapters, could only have been added a century and a
half later (see p. 113), "when the recollection of the
authorship of this section having been forgotten, it
could, not unnaturally, be appended to the writings of
Isaiah." So the critics first dissect Isaiah, and then
find it impossible to get the disjointed pieces together
again without putting the collection of the canon at a
date at variance with historical testimony and every reliable indication bearing on the subject. It is, indeed,
a puzzling question which the critics have to solve, and
to which no satisfactory answer can be given, how it
came to pass that this prince of prophets, living, as we
are told, near the end of the exile, whose predictions of
the coming deliverance and the rebuilding of Jerusalem
and the temple were so strikingly fulfilled, and who must
have stirred the souls of the exiles to an unwonted degree with his own glowing enthusiasm, could be so utterly unknown, and not only his name, but his very existence so entirely forgotten, that his prophecies were
attributed to another, who lived at a different period
of time, and under entirely different circumstances.
But if the exigencies of the critical hypothesis demand a long interval to account for this complete
oblivion, does it follow that the recognition of the divine authority of this magnificent prophecy was so
delayed?

(3.) It has been claimed[1] that Zech. ix.–xiv. was not

[1] Dillmann, p. 450 ; Ryle, p. 106, who nevertheless, p. 101, quotes
Zech. xiii. 3 as the language of Zechariah. Strack, Real-Encyk., vii.,
p. 422.

written by Zechariah, but by some unknown prophet, and was placed at the end of the Minor Prophets before Malachi had been added to the collection. It would thus stand immediately after Zechariah, and so came ultimately to be attached to that book. This is urged as showing that the canon was formed by a gradual process. But if all this were so, it would only prove that the canon was formed and the collection of Minor Prophets made before Malachi was written, to which, of course, it was then immediately added; and it effectually disposes of those critical conjectures which would put Joel, Jonah or Zech. ix.–xiv. after the time of Malachi.

(4.) The critics fix the final closing of the collection of the prophets by their notion of the time when the Book of Daniel was written. Thus Wildeboer (p. 116): " At what time the division of the prophets was closed we are not informed. But on account of Dan. ix. 2, whose author, living about 165 B.C., seems to know ' the books ' as a collection with definite limits, and because the Book of Daniel itself was unable to obtain a place in the second section, we fix as a terminus *ad quem* about 200 B.C." [1] But we have already seen that the Book of Daniel has its rightful place in the third division of the canon, uninfluenced by the question whether at the time of its insertion the second division was open or closed ; and that the date, which the critics assign to the book, is determined by presuppositions in regard to miracles and prophecy, which we do not share; and that apart from these presuppositions there is no valid reason for discrediting the claim which it makes for itself, confirmed by the belief of all past ages and by the testimony of our Lord, that its author was no other than Daniel himself.

(5.) Wildeboer tells us (p. 123) : " When the conscious-

[1] So Ryle, p. 112.

ness had become general that no more prophets would
appear, the prophetic writings were collected and added
to the collection of the Nebiim [historical books of the
prophets], which had been in existence since the days of
Nehemiah.   It is quite possible that the memory of the
interval between the canonization of the historical
books and of the prophetic writings proper is perpetuated by the order of the two groups of books and by
the appellation based upon it, Former and Latter
Prophets." This idea that prophetic writings were not
regarded as canonical, until there were no longer any
prophets among the people, is as arbitrary and unfounded as the opposite opinion, which figures so
largely in the reasonings of the critics that "the incorporation of recent or almost contemporary work in the
same collection with the older prophets" would not
have been approved.[1] The living prophet did not su-
persede his predecessor of a former age, nor did the
older prophets diminish the authority or destroy the
value of those of recent date. The question was one of
divine commission and authority, not of antiquity, nor
of the form of delivery, whether oral or written.

We have now reviewed all the considerations of any
moment, that are urged by the critics in defence of their
position, that the books of the prophets were not admitted to the canon until long after the public recognition of the binding obligation of the law in the time of
Ezra. And we have found nothing to militate against
the belief that the writings of the prophets, delivered
to the people as a declaration of the divine will, possessed canonical authority from the moment of their
appearance. Thus the canon grew with each successive
issue, until the last was published, when the canon was
complete. The second division of the canon was ac-

[1] Ryle, Canon, p. 106.

cordingly completed by Malachi, the last of the prophets who was a contemporary of Nehemiah.

How was it with the K'thubhim? It has been maintained [1] (1) that no steps were taken toward the formation of a third division, and none of the books found in it were admitted to the canon until the second division had first been closed. And this, it is alleged, could not have taken place until a considerable time after Malachi, when the general conviction had been reached that prophecy had altogether ceased, and no more prophets were to be expected. This is argued on the ground that Ezra, Nehemiah, and Chronicles would have been put in the same division with the other historical books such as Samuel and Kings, and Daniel with Isaiah, Jeremiah, and Ezekiel, if that division had not been already closed, when they were accepted as canonical. But it has already been shown that in the Hebrew canon the books are not classified according to the character of their contents, but by the official status of their authors. Books written by prophets stand in the second division; those written by inspired men, not belong-

---

[1] So Bertholdt, p. 81; DeWette, § 13; Robertson Smith, p. 179. Dillmann, pp. 455, 469, distinguishes between the older K'thubhim, as Psalms, Proverbs, Job, and the Song of Solomon, and the more recent, as Chronicles with Ezra, Esther, Ecclesiastes, and Daniel. The former were, in his opinion, held in very high esteem from the early period after the exile, but were not yet in the full sense of the word canonical. Bleek (pp. 666–668) holds this same view with regard to the Psalms, but is more doubtful about Proverbs, Job, and the Song of Solomon, although he believes that they were then undoubtedly in existence. Ryle (p. 121) thinks that some of the K'thubhim were "an informal appendix to the canon of the law and the prophets" prior to their own canonization. Wildeboer says (p. 138): "Probably most of the Kethubhim were already in existence when the prophets were canonized," and "many of them were originally united with prophetic books. When the earlier scribes secured canonical authority for the prophets, 'the rest of the books' remained as a group of indefinite extent."

ing to the prophetic order in its strict and proper sense, were assigned to the third division. There is no need, therefore, for assuming that the prophets were closed and could not be reopened, when these books were introduced into the canon, in order to account for the position which they occupy.

(2.) It is asserted that several of the K'thubhim are of much later date than the time of Ezra, and particularly that the Book of Daniel was not written until B.C. 168 or 167.[1] It has already been shown that this assertion is unfounded. The time allowed for a book to gain credence, which first made its appearance in the period of the Maccabees, but claimed to be the work of the Prophet Daniel, who lived three centuries and a half before, is remarkably short. Mattathias, who died B.C. 167, encouraged his sons by examples drawn from this book, Hananiah, Mishael, and Azariah in the fiery furnace and Daniel in the den of lions (1 Macc. ii. 59, 60). There is also a plain reference to Dan. ix. 27, xii. 11 in 1 Macc. i. 54. And in B.C. 130, as attested by the Prologue to Ecclesiasticus, all the books of the canon had been translated into Greek, and Daniel, of course, among them. And according to the uniform admission of all the critics, this book would not have found admission to the canon if it had not been believed to be the genuine work of the Prophet Daniel.

(3.) In the order of books in the Hebrew Bible Chronicles[2] stands last, and is preceded by Ezra and Nehemiah. As Ezra is supposed, not without reason, to have been a continuation of Chronicles, it is argued that Ezra must have been separated and admitted to the

---

[1] So Driver; Ryle, p. 112, and Wildeboer, pp. 27, 143, say B.C. 165.

[2] In the Massoretic arrangement Chronicles is the first book of the K'thubhim.

canon before Chronicles was received.[1] But there is no reason to suppose that the order of these books indicates the order of their reception into the canon. If that had been so, Daniel should have stood last according to the critical hypothesis of its origin. In the K'thubhim the three large books, Psalms, Proverbs, Job, stand first, then the five Megilloth, then Daniel, Ezra, Nehemiah in chronological order, and finally Chronicles as a sort of historical appendix, reviewing the entire period from the creation to the end of the exile.

(4.) Dillmann (p. 483) argues that the additions to Esther and Daniel in the Greek, and the recasting of Chronicles and Ezra in the apocryphal Esdras show that these books were not regarded as inviolable as the law and the prophets. But the legends connected with the law in the later Targums prove that its canonical authority was no bar to imaginative additions suited to the popular taste. And it is not strange that histories so remarkable as those of Esther and Daniel should be particularly alluring to those who were given to flights of fancy.

There is nothing in all this to support the contention of the critics that the three divisions of the canon represent three distinct collections made at widely separated periods; and nothing to weaken the evidence afforded by the orderly distribution of books into classes, that the arrangement was made at some one time and upon a definite plan.

It must be remembered that the canonization of books is not to be confounded with their collection. Books were not made canonical by the act of some public authority, such as a decision rendered in their favor by an assembly of scribes or doctors or a general council

---

[1] This notion is distinctly rejected by Buhl, Kanon und Text, p. 39.

of the nation. This would be to attribute to the Jewish Church in its organized capacity a power which even Bellarmin,[1] disposed as he was to magnify ecclesiastical prerogatives to the utmost, did not venture to claim for the Christian Church. The canon does not derive its authority from the Church, whether Jewish or Christian; the office of the Church is merely that of a custodian and a witness. The collection of the canon is simply bringing together into one volume those books whose sacred character has already secured general acknowledgment. And the universal acceptance of the collection at the time, and subsequently, shows that it truly represents the current belief of the Jewish people, formed when they were still under prophetic guidance.[2]

[1] "Ecclesiam nullo modo posse facere librum canonicum de non canonico, nec contra, sed tantum declarare, quis sit habendus canonicus, et hoc non temere, nec pro arbitratu, sed ex veterum testimoniis et similitudine librorum, de quibus ambigitur, cum illis de quibus non ambigitur, ac demun ex communi sensu et quasi gustu populi Christiani."—Bellarmin, De Verbo Dei, Lib. I., c. 10, n. 16.

[2] Wildeboer (p. 165) concludes his dissertation by what seems like a claim of orthodox endorsement of the modern critical theory of the canon: "As long ago as the beginning of the eighteenth century, a learned and pious German theologian, and a champion of orthodoxy too, wrote these true words: 'Canon non uno, quod dicunt, actu ab hominibus, sed paulatim a Deo, animorum temporumque rectore, productus est.'" This same passage had been before quoted by Strack, and from him adopted by Driver, p. x, and by Ryle conspicuously placed opposite the title-page as the motto of his volume. It is an absolute perversion of Loescher's meaning to represent his words as in any way sanctioning the critical theory that the books of the Old Testament only attained canonical authority by slow degrees centuries after they were written, and that this was first given to them by some public official act, successively performed for each of the divisions of the canon. The entire passage, from which the words above cited are taken, reads as follows (Keil's Introduction, 2d Ed., Eng. Trans., II., p. 152): "There existed from the age of Moses canonical books, from their internal light and dignity esteemed as divine from their first appearance, which were laid up in the former temple in the ark of the

We have no positive information when or by whom the sacred books were collected and arranged. The canon was completed by Malachi, the last of the prophets, probably about 425 B.C. The first authentic statement on the subject after this time is found in the Prologue to Ecclesiasticus, which was written about 132 B.C.[1] It is there spoken of as a definite and well-known

covenant. To these others, recognized as divine from the time that they were written and publicly read, were gradually added, not by the judgment of Ezra or the Synagogue, or by decrees of Council or Synod (Sanhedrim), but by the universal acceptance and usage of the whole Church, until by the Book of Malachi the canon was closed. For prophets ceased at that time, the use of the sacred tongue ceased, in place of which the language of the Targums, the Greek, and the Rabbinical were substituted. Hence the ancient Jewish Church acknowledged none of the books written afterward as divine and belonging to the Mikdash (Sanctuary); *and so the canon itself was produced, not by one act of men, so to speak, but gradually by God, who controls minds and seasons.*"

[1] The date assigned to this Prologue and to the Book of Ecclesiasticus, to which it is prefixed, depends upon the statement in the Prologue that the writer of it came into Egypt "in the thirty-eighth year in the reign of Euergetes." There were two kings of this name in Egypt, Ptolemy Euergetes I., who reigned twenty-five years, B.C. 246–221, and Ptolemy Physcon, who also gave himself the cognomen of Euergetes II., and who reigned twenty-nine years, B.C. 145–116. A clew has also been sought in what is said of " Simon, the high-priest, the son of Onias " (Ecclus. 1). Singularly enough there were also two of this name who filled the office of high-priest, Simon I., B.C. 300–287, and Simon II., B.C. 226–198. Two different views have accordingly been taken of the date of the Prologue. One, that Euergetes I. is intended, and the thirty-eighth year of the writer's life, so that the Prologue must have been written somewhere between B.C. 246 and 221, and the Book of Ecclesiasticus about fifty years earlier. The other and more commonly received view is based on the fact that Euergetes II. was for a time associated in the kingdom with his brother Ptolemy Philometor. If his reign is reckoned from B.C. 170, the beginning of this joint sovereignty, his thirty-eighth year will be B.C. 132. The form of expression employed to denote the thirty-eighth year of Euergetes, though unusual, has analogies in Hag. i. 1; Zech. i. 7, vii. 1; 1 Macc. xiv. 27.

body of writings in three divisions, severally denominated "the law and the prophets and the rest of the
books." When and by whom they were collected the
writer does not state, but it must have been before the
time of his grandfather, Jesus, the son of Sirach, circ.
B.C. 180, who was the author of the book, and of whom
he speaks as a diligent reader of "the law and the
prophets and the other books of the fathers."

The critics are at great pains to weaken the force of
this testimony to the third division of the canon. Thus
Dillmann (p. 478) : "At that time a third series of highly
prized writings had already been formed, which about
corresponds with our third canon. But that this series
contained only and entirely the same books, which
stand in our third canon, can never be proved from these
expressions, and therefore the passage cannot avail as a
witness for a closed canon." Ryle (p. 143) : "The vague-
ness of the writer's words in designating the third division stands in sharp contrast to the precision with
which he describes the first two divisions by the very
names that have traditionally been attached to them."
Wildeboer (p. 33): "He cannot have meant an indefinite
number. But though he may have been well aware
what books were included in it, he has not told us, and
so has left us in uncertainty." There is no more "vague-
ness" in the expression employed to denote the third
division than in the other two ; and no more reason for
"uncertainty" as to the number of books contained in
it, than those contained in the law or the prophets. According to the testimony of Josephus, nothing had been
added to the sacred books or taken from them since the
reign of Artaxerxes. The uniform belief of the Jews
was that the Holy Spirit had departed from Israel after
Malachi. The statement in the Prologue is precisely in
accord with this. The language is just what might be

expected if the canon had been definitely settled for three centuries; and there is nothing to suggest the suspicion that the third division was still in the process of formation. Of this there is no proof whatever. The long interval between Malachi and the son of Sirach affords the critics a chance for endless theorizing and confident assertions, which are, after all, purely conjectural and destitute of any real foundation.

Beyond the statements now considered we have nothing but legends and uncertain traditions in relation to the process by which, the time when, or the persons by whom the sacred books were put together as we already find them in the time of the son of Sirach. Whatever interest may attach to this question, it is plain that it does not in any measure affect the authority of the sacred writings. This is in nowise dependent upon their being gathered together. A book inspired of God is just as authoritative in its separate state as it is when united with other books of like character. And a book not inspired of God has no more right to control our faith, when mingled with books really inspired, than if it stood alone.

In 2 Esdras, an apocryphal book full of fables, and dating probably from the close of the first century of the Christian era, it is said (xiv. 21 ff.) that the law (by which is meant the entire Scriptures) was burned at the time that the temple was destroyed, but Ezra was enabled by divine inspiration to restore it. In the course of forty days he dictated ninety-four [1] books; seventy of which were to be delivered only to the wise, and the others were to be published openly for all to read. As twenty-four is the number of the canonical books, as commonly reckoned by the Jews, it is evident that these are the

---

[1] So the Ethiopic Version, and this is probably the true reading; the Vulgate has 204, and some copies 904.

books to be given to the public. The same legend, shorn of some of its particulars, is found in quite a number of the early Christian fathers, as Clemens Alexandrinus, Tertullian, Irenæus [1] and others, who relate that the Scriptures perished in the destruction of Jerusalem by Nebuchadnezzar, but Ezra was divinely inspired to restore them perfectly, and did so without the slightest loss or alteration. This fabulous story is, of course, entitled to no credence. It is not unlikely, however, that it may be so far founded on fact as that Ezra took a prominent part in the collection and arrangement of the sacred books after the exile, and in multiplying copies for general circulation.

Another tradition relating to this subject is found in 2 Macc. ii. 13. Critics have been greatly divided in opinion as to the degree of credit to be attached to this passage. Some treat it as entirely trustworthy, others as undeserving of attention. It is in a spurious letter purporting to be written by Jews in Jerusalem and in Judea to those in Egypt, and is professedly based on "writings and memorabilia of Nehemiah," of which nothing whatever is known. It says that "Nehemiah founding a library, gathered together the books concerning the kings and prophets, and those of David, and letters of kings concerning consecrated gifts." No mention is here made of the law, which had been spoken of in ver. 2 as given by Jeremiah to those who were carried into exile. To this Nehemiah added " the [books] concerning the kings and the prophets," by which are obviously meant the historical and prophetical books,

---

[1] Hävernick, Einleitung, p. 44, and Keil, Einleitung, p. 544, claim that the testimony of Irenæus adv. Haer., III., 21, is independent of 2 Esdras, and simply attributes to Ezra the collection of the canon; but Oehler, p. 246, and Strack, p. 415, have shown, from a consideration of the entire passage, that this is a mistake.

here classed together as forming the second division of the canon. Finally certain prominent parts of the third and last division, which may or may not be put for the whole, viz., "the [writings] of David," *i.e.*, the Psalms and "letters of kings concerning consecrated gifts," which can only refer to the letters of the Persian monarchs contained in the Book of Ezra.[1]

In ver. 14 it is added, "In like manner also Judas" Maccabeus, who is represented (i. 10) as uniting with others in sending this letter, "gathered together all those things that were lost by reason of the war." It is known from other sources that Antiochus Epiphanes made a desperate attempt to destroy the sacred books.[2] These were carefully regathered by Judas in the same manner as before. This letter further contains the legend of the miraculous preservation of the sacred fire (i. 18 ff.) and of the tabernacle, the ark, and the altar of incense (ii. 4 ff.). This curious compound of truth and fable attributes to Nehemiah an agency in collecting the sacred writings which, in itself considered, is altogether credible.

These intimations from legendary sources acquire greater significance from the fact that they are corroborated by other and independent considerations. Thus:

1. Ezra is repeatedly and with emphasis called "the scribe" (Neh. viii. 1, 4, 9, 13, xii. 26, 36); "a ready scribe in the law of Moses" (Ezra vii. 6); "a scribe of the words of the commandments of Jehovah, and of his stat-

---

[1] Wildeboer, p. 117, limits "the books concerning the kings and prophets" to "the prophetico-historical" to the exclusion of the prophetical books; Movers, p. 15, applies this expression to Chronicles. Bertholdt, I., p. 76, understands "the books of David" to mean the Books of Samuel. Wildeboer, p. 39, overlooks entirely the sacred character of the collection, and says that Nehemiah "as a lover of books founded a library."

[2] 1 Macc. i. 56, 57; Josephus, Ant., xii. 5, 4.

utes to Israel " (ver. 11); " a scribe of the law of the God
of heaven " (vs. 12, 22), a character in which he was
known, as appears from the passages last cited, before
he went up from the captivity. It hence appears that
his professional occupation was with the Scriptures, as
a student and interpreter, and engaged probably in the
preparation of copies for the use of the people and in
certifying their correctness. From Ezra dates the origin
of that race of scribes so distinguished subsequently,
and so frequently alluded to in the New Testament as
men learned in the law, the custodians and conservators
of the sacred text.

2. The period immediately succeeding the exile was
devoted to the single task of restoring everything after
the model of former times. It is well known how ac-
tively and earnestly Ezra was engaged in the reinstitu-
tion of the temple service and in reviving the old arrangements of the theocracy in accordance with the
prescriptions of Moses, David, and Solomon, and what
pains he took to have the people made acquainted with
the law of Moses and in general with all the ancient
regulations and statutes of divine authority. The
thoughts of all dwelt upon the glories of Israel in the
past, and their highest hope was to have them repro-
duced in their own experience. The history of God's
dealings with their fathers and the revelations made to
them were prominently before their minds, and formed
the burden of their supplications (Neh. ix.). It is just
what might be expected from the needs and longings of
the time, and from the nature of the work to which Ezra
so energetically addressed himself, that the sacred writings would then be carefully gathered for the guidance
and instruction of the people, and for their own more
secure preservation and transmission.

3. Private and partial collections of these writings had

already been formed, and were in the possession of individuals. This is apparent from the frequent references made by the prophets, such as Jeremiah and Ezekiel, to the language of their predecessors or to the former history of the nation, from the explicit mention of a prediction of Micah, delivered a century before, by the elders in addressing the people (Jer. xxvi. 17–19), and from "the books" of which Daniel (ix. 2) speaks at the close of the captivity, and in which the prophecies of Jeremiah must have been included. These would naturally suggest the formation of a public and complete collection, and would prepare the way for it.

4. All the books of the Old Testament were already written in the time of Ezra and Nehemiah, so that there was nothing to prevent their collection of them. The last addition to the canon was made by Malachi, a contemporary of Nehemiah. That a large proportion of the books of the canon were then in existence is universally acknowledged. The law and the prophets and several of the K'thubhim, it is generally admitted, were already written. No one disputes this with regard to the great majority of the Psalms; and there is no good reason why all may not have been written by the end of the first century after the exile. It has been plausibly argued from 1 Chron. xvi. 35, 36, where the doxology is inserted, which marks the conclusion of the fourth Book of the Psalter (Ps. cvi. 48), that the Psalms must have been completed and arranged as at present before Chronicles was written. Proverbs, as is expressly stated (xxv. 1), was completed in the reign of Hezekiah. And in regard to those books, which the critics assign to a late postexilic date, it has already been shown that they do so on insufficient grounds.

5. The cessation of prophecy seems to be foreshadowed by Zechariah (xiii. 2–5), who speaks of the time as

coming when the assumption of the office of a prophet shall be evidence of deception. And perhaps by Malachi (iv. 5), who only looks forward to the coming of Elijah before the personal appearance of the Lord. That succeeding generations were fully aware that there was no prophet among them is plain from 1 Macc. iv. 46, ix. 27, xiv. 41, which speak of the perplexity arising from the absence of a prophet, and the postponement of questions for decision by one, if any should arise. This shows how clearly the divine was discriminated from what was purely human, and creates a presumption that the inspired writings were not only sundered from all uninspired productions, as they have been from the beginning, but were regarded as a complete whole to which no further addition could be made. Their collection could scarcely have been delayed beyond the time when it was felt that the line of prophets was coming to an end.

These considerations, taken in connection with the legends and traditions previously recited, whose existence is to be accounted for, and can thus be most satisfactorily explained, make it highly probable that the canon was collected by Ezra and Nehemiah, or in their time.

VIII

THE EXTENT OF THE CANON—THE CANON OF THE JEWS

WE have now considered the formation and collection of the Old Testament canon. Our next inquiry concerns its compass or extent. What books belong to this canon? And how can they be identified and distinguished from all others? This topic will be treated under three heads, and in the following order:

1. The canon of the Jews.
2. The canon of Christ and his Apostles.
3. The canon of the Christian Church.

The Jews in all parts of the world accept the same canon, which is found without variation in all copies of the Hebrew Bible. This unanimity is found to exist as far back as the constituents of the Old Testament can be traced.

The Talmudic tract Baba Bathra, which is attributed to Judas Hakkadosh in the second century A.D., contains a catalogue of the sacred books. They are there classed in three divisions as in our modern Hebrew Bibles, viz., five books of the law, eight of the prophets, and eleven of the K'thubhim, making a total of twenty-four. In this enumeration the whole of Samuel is counted one book, so is Kings, and so is Chronicles. The twelve Minor Prophets are also reckoned one, and Nehemiah is included under Ezra as forming with it one book. Under the last two divisions the books are arranged in the following order, which differs somewhat from that which is customary in the Hebrew Bible:

The Prophets: 1, Joshua; 2, Judges; 3, Samuel; 4, Kings; 5, Jeremiah; 6, Ezekiel; 7, Isaiah; 8, The Twelve.

The K'thubhim: 1, Ruth; 2, Psalms; 3, Job; 4, Proverbs; 5, Ecclesiastes; 6, Song of Songs; 7, Lamentations; 8, Daniel; 9, Esther; 10, Ezra; 11, Chronicles.

Another native testimony, a century earlier, is found in a passage already quoted (p. 37) from the historian Josephus, "Against Apion," i. 8. His statement respecting the sacred books is not so explicit as that of the Talmud, since he does not mention them by name; but he gives their number, and describes them so that it can without difficulty be determined which they were. He gives both a different total and a different classification from that of the Talmud; the difference, however, lies not in the contents of the canon, but in the mode of enumeration. We have before seen (p. 87) that the books of the canon were reckoned 24 if Ruth and Lamentations were counted as separate books, but 22 if Ruth was attached to Judges and Lamentations to Jeremiah. The Talmud adopts the former reckoning, Josephus the latter. These 22 books he divides into three classes: 1, five books of Moses; 2, thirteen books of the prophets, who wrote what was done in their times from the death of Moses to the reign of Artaxerxes, the successor of Xerxes, king of Persia; 3, four books containing hymns to God and counsels for men for the conduct of life. The five books of Moses are easily recognized. The other books are readily made out by comparison of the catalogue already given from the Talmud. The four containing hymns to God and counsels for men are unquestionably 1, Psalms; 2,

Proverbs; 3, Ecclesiastes; 4, The Song of Solomon.
The thirteen books of the prophets must then be

1. Joshua.	8. Job.
2. Judges, including Ruth.	9. Isaiah.
3. Samuel.	10. Jeremiah and Lamenta-
4. Kings.	tions.
5. Chronicles.	11. Ezekiel.
6. Ezra, with Nehemiah.	12. Daniel.
7. Esther.	13. The Minor Prophets.[1]

It will be observed that Josephus here departs from
the current classification, and adopts one of his own,
suited to his immediate purpose. He is defending the
historical trustworthiness of the books of his nation, and
accordingly arranges them from a historical point of
view: the books of Moses, containing the history from
the creation to his own death; then the other books having any historical material, which he refers to prophets
in the wide sense of men divinely inspired; and finally
those which are not historical in their character, but
contain hymns and wise counsels.

The canon of Josephus might also, without the aid of
the Talmud, be constructed almost entirely out of his
own writings. In the course of his writings he mentions nearly every book in the Old Testament, either

---

[1] J. D. Michaelis contended that the four books of the third division
were Job, Psalms, Proverbs, and Ecclesiastes, and that the Song of
Solomon was not included in the canon of Josephus, Or. u. Ex. Bib.,
III., p. 47. Oeder excluded Esther, Ezra with Nehemiah, and Chron-
icles from the list, and made up the number by separating Ruth from
Judges, and counting the two books of Samuel and the two of Kings
separately, Or. u. Ex. Bib., II., p. 2t. Haneberg did the same, Theol.
Quartalschrift for 1855, p. 69. Movers, Canon, pp. 27, 31, excludes
Esther and counts Ezra and Nehemiah separately. Graetz rejects
Ecclesiastes and the Song of Solomon and counts in Ruth and Lamentations, Kohelet, p. 169. These fanciful suggestions are of no account, and it is now generally admitted that the canon of Josephus
is identical with that of the Hebrew Bible.

explicitly ranking them among the sacred books, or quoting and making use of them in such a way as shows that they belong to the number above described.[1] The only books which he does not thus mention or make use of are Job, Proverbs, Ecclesiastes, and Solomon's Song. The reason why these are not quoted by him in the same manner as the rest, is not because he did not rate them as of equal authority, but simply because they did not furnish any materials which he had occasion to use in his histories. Job was outside of the line of the chosen people, and had no connection, therefore, with the ancient history of the Jews. And the other three books are not of a historical character. But that he accepted them as canonical is evident from the fact that they are needed to make up the number 22, which he assigns to the sacred books.

This concurrent testimony of the Talmud and Josephus with regard to the Jewish canon might, if it were necessary, be confirmed by statements of early Christian fathers, who made special inquiry into this matter, and have left catalogues of the books esteemed sacred by the Jews. The native authorities already examined are, however, sufficient to determine this point; and the statements of the fathers will more naturally find their place in an account of the canon of the Old Testament as it has been received and held in the Christian Church.

The question has here been raised whether the canon attested by Josephus and the Talmud was universally acknowledged by the Jews. The Samaritans, as has been before stated, accepted only the books of Moses.[2]

---

[1] Eichhorn shows this in detail, pointing out the passages in which each book is referred to or made use of, and the manner in which it is spoken of.—Rep. für Morg. Litt., V., pp. 260–270.

[2] The modern Samaritans are also in possession of a chronicle called

They had a temple of their own on Mount Gerizim, and refused to acknowledge any book of the Old Testament which sanctioned any other place of worship. Some of the early Christian fathers alleged that the Sadducees admitted no other sacred books than those of Moses. This is, however, a mistake into which they may have been betrayed by confounding the Sadducees with the Samaritans, with whom they had no connection whatever. The proofs adduced of so restricted a canon of the Sadducees are devoid of force. Some passages in Josephus have been appealed to ("Antiq.," xiii. 10, 6, xviii. 1, 4), which, however, speak not of their rejection of any of the books of Scripture, but only of the traditions of the Pharisees. Their denial of a resurrection (Acts xxiii. 8) does not prove their rejection of those Scriptures in which it is taught (*e.g.*, Dan. xii. 2), any more than their disbelief in the existence of angels disproves their acceptance of the Pentateuch. They doubtless managed to put some different interpretation upon passages whose obvious sense they were reluctant to accept. Nor does the fact that our Lord proves the doctrine of the resurrection against them by a citation from the Book of Exodus (Mat. xxii. 23–32), when clearer proofs could have been found in later portions of the Old Testament, sanction the view that they acknowledged only the inspiration and authority of the Pentateuch.[1] In this case our Lord would more likely

the book of Joshua, which has but a slight connection with the genuine book of that name, and professes to give the history from the time of Joshua to that of the Roman emperors.

[1] Lightfoot, Hebrew and Talmudical Exercitations on John iv. 25, adduces a passage from the Talmud in which R. Gamaliel argues with a Sadducee for the resurrection from the law, the prophets and the K'thubhim, quoting in proof Isaiah and the Song of Solomon. "The books themselves out of which these proofs were brought were not excepted against, but the places quoted had another sense put upon

have rebuked them for their rejection of so large a portion of the word of God, as on other occasions he condemns the Pharisees for making it void by their traditions. And our Saviour's urging the passage from Exodus in preference to others may have been both to show that this doctrine pervaded the Scriptures even from the earliest periods, and also to bring the authority of the great legislator upon the case, who stood in a unique position among the inspired men of the former economy from the peculiar intimacy to which he was admitted by Jehovah, and the lofty rank belonging to him as the founder of that dispensation. Just as special stress might be laid upon the words of Jesus in some matter of faith or duty without at all implying that the canon of the New Testament was limited to the Gospels, or that the writings of the apostles were not of binding authority.

There is also reason to believe that the peculiar sects of contemplative ascetics or mystics, the Essenes and the Therapeutæ, accepted the same canon as the people at large, though they also had other books written by members of their own sect which were held in high esteem.[1]

It was confidently affirmed by Semler and Corrodi, and has been maintained by others since, that the Alexandrian Jews had a more comprehensive canon than the Jews of Palestine; and appeal is made to the Septuagint Version, which contained books not in the Hebrew Bible, and to the esteem in which these books were held by some of the early Christians. But there is satisfactory evidence that these supernumerary books were no more regarded as belonging to the canon in the one place than they were in the other.

them." A Sadducee is also mentioned, who quotes the prophet Amos. See also Herzfeld, III., p. 104.
[1] Hävernick, Einleitung, I., pp. 75, 76.

1. There is a strong antecedent presumption against a difference of canon in the two places. To alter the canon would be to change the very basis of their religion. Such an act on the part of the Egyptian Jews would create a breach between them and their co-religionists in the Holy Land. And there are abundant indications that they were solicitous to cement their intercourse with them, and to maintain their standing as orthodox Jews. Jerusalem was the centre to which the Jews resorted from every quarter. It set the standard which was everywhere followed. Philo speaks of his having been commissioned by his brethren in Egypt to offer in their name and on their behalf in the Temple at Jerusalem; and this was most probably in accordance with a usual custom.

2. The translator of the Book of Ecclesiasticus into Greek, in the Prologue before spoken of, makes mention both of the sacred books which his grandfather had studied in Palestine, and of those which he himself found in Egypt translated into Greek; and he uses precisely the same expressions in regard to both, naming both under the same threefold division of "the law, the prophets and the rest of the books," and without intimating that there was any difference between them.

3. The account of the sacred books given by Josephus is found in a treatise written by him against Apion, a grammarian of Alexandria. And if the canon received by Jews resident in Egypt was different from that of Palestine, it is unaccountable that he should have made no allusion to that circumstance.

4. Philo (flor. A.D. 41) was an Alexandrian Jew of great eminence, and the only one whose writings have been preserved. He makes repeated reference to the books of the Old Testament and comments largely upon particular portions of them. Unfortunately he has no-

where left a list of the books esteemed sacred by his countrymen, nor has he even furnished such a general description of them as is found in Josephus. But the incidental allusions and references to individual books and the statements regarding them in different parts of his writings have been carefully collected, and from them the canon of Philo can be pretty well made out, and shown to be identical with that of Josephus and the Talmud. According to the detailed account given by Eichhorn[1] all the books of the Old Testament are either expressly spoken of as inspired, or else quoted or distinctly mentioned, except Esther, Ezekiel, Daniel, Ecclesiastes and the Song of Solomon.[2] He does not happen to have made any allusion to these books, as he had no occasion to do so ; but their canonicity in Alexandria as well as elsewhere is sufficiently established by other testimonies. At the same time it is to be observed that Philo never quotes nor mentions any one of the apocryphal books, though there are indications that he was acquainted with them. So total a silence on his part is not consistent with his classing them among the sacred books. As Eichhorn remarks, " He does not even show them the respect which he shows to Plato, Philolaus, Solon, Hippocrates, Heraclitus and others, from whose writings he often adduces passages."

[1] In the Rep. Bib. u. Morg. Litt., V., pp. 238–250, based upon Hornemann, Observationes ad illustrationem doctrinæ de canone V. T. ex Philone, 1775.

[2] Hornemann includes Chronicles among the books omitted by Philo, but Buhl (Canon, p. 17) and Pick (Journal of the Exegetical Society, 1884, p. 129) show that it is cited by him. Only two of the Minor Prophets, Hosea and Zechariah, are quoted; but as The Twelve were in all ancient catalogues reckoned one book, the citation of any part shows the esteem in which the whole was held. So Ruth was reckoned part of Judges, Lamentations of Jeremiah, and Nehemiah of Ezra; and though they are not separately mentioned, their canonicity is implied.

It is urged, however, that the presence of several books in the Septuagint Version which are not in the Hebrew Bible, proves that these books were esteemed a part of the canon in Egypt, where this version was prepared. This is the most plausible argument that can be advanced in favor of a more comprehensive canon in Alexandria than in Palestine; and yet it is after all only an argument addressed to our ignorance. For,

1. The origin and early history of the Septuagint Version, and even its original compass, are involved in great obscurity. It is evident from the various merit and ability with which different parts of it are executed, that it was not all prepared at one time nor by one body of translators. No one can tell when the entire translation was finished and put together, nor when and how these other writings came to be associated with it.[1]

2. As is correctly stated by Wildeboer, p. 35, "All the manuscripts of the LXX. which we possess are of Christian origin, so that in some even the Magnificat of Mary appears among the hymns. On this account we cannot always say positively whether we have before us the views of the Alexandrians. . . . In the various manuscripts the number of apocryphal books varies, hence no established list existed."[2]

---

[1] Cosin, p. 54, quotes Cyril of Jerusalem, "Read the divine Scriptures, namely the twenty-two books of the Old Testament, which the seventy-two interpreters translated." According to Cyril, therefore, the Septuagint Version proper contained only the twenty-two books of the Hebrew canon.

[2] To the same purport, Ryle, p. 169 : "The manuscripts of the LXX. are, all of them, of Christian origin; and moreover differ from one another in the arrangement as well as in the selection of the books. There is no uniform Alexandrian list. The Christian Church derived their Old Testament Scriptures from the Jews ; but whether they found the books of the Apocrypha in Jewish copies, or added them afterwards, we have no means of judging."

3. The connection of these books with the Septuagint must, of course, be explained in conformity with the proofs already given of the identity of the canon in Alexandria and Jerusalem. It seems most probable that these books were gradually attached to the Greek Bible as a sort of supplement or appendix, which, though not of canonical authority, stood in an intimate relation to the Scriptures, as connected with the later history of the chosen people, or as suggestive of devout meditations, and thus widely separated from all profane or merely secular writings. As late as the second century A.D. it was customary in Palestine to write each of the books of the Old Testament on a separate manuscript, instead of combining all or a number of them in the same volume. If a similar practice prevailed in Alexandria, it is easy to see how these related though uncanonical books might at first have been laid alongside of the sacred books for safe keeping; and ultimately, when the practice arose of including several books in the same volume, these extraneous books might have been copied along with the rest, and joined to those to which they seemed to be most nearly related.

It is further urged that the apocryphal books found in the Septuagint were accepted by Christian fathers as of divine authority, which could only be because they derived them from the Jews. And as the Jews of Palestine did not receive them, it must have been from the Jews of Alexandria that the fathers learned to hold them in such high esteem. This can only receive a satisfactory reply when the history of the canon in the Christian Church is under consideration. It will then appear that, however unadvisedly some of the fathers may have expressed themselves in this matter, these books were not placed on a par with the Hebrew Scriptures in the early church.

An argument has also been drawn from an obviously erroneous reading in the prologues of Jerome to Tobit and Judith, in which he is made to say that these books were ranked by the Jews among the Hagiographa; and as these books were not canonical in Palestine, it has been inferred that he must have had reference to the Jews of Alexandria. But Jerome elsewhere explicitly asserts that these books formed no part of the canon of the Jews; the best authorities are, therefore, agreed that "Hagiographa" is an error in transcription, and the true reading is "Apocrypha."

Wildeboer maintains that there was no strictly defined canon in Alexandria. He says, p. 33: "The addition of apocryphal pieces, and even whole books, which are in no way distinguished from the other writings, shows that the Alexandrians knew no fixed canon." And, p. 35: "It must not be assumed that the existence of an official Palestinian canon was known in Alexandria. . . . The Law was translated first and most faithfully. . . . The translation of the Prophets was of later origin, and is already freer; that of the Hagiographa is the freest of all. From this it may reasonably be inferred that the Alexandrian translators themselves held the Prophets and Hagiographa in less exalted an esteem than the Law." And, pp. 36, 37: "Philo entertained such a conception of divine inspiration as to exclude the idea that he accepted an officially defined inspired canon. . . . Inspiration, according to him, is by no means confined to the Sacred Scriptures. He regards it as obtainable by any one that practises virtue."

It has already been shown how the existence of additional books in the Septuagint can be explained consistently with the acknowledgment of a more limited canon by the Jews of Alexandria. What is said of the

Law being more exactly translated than the Prophets, and the Prophets than the Hagiographa, is just as true of the Palestinian Targums as of the Alexandrian Septuagint; and if it disproves a fixed and definite canon in Alexandria, it does the same in Palestine. A stricter regard for the letter of the Law than of the Prophets is quite conceivable without disparagement to the canonicity of the latter. And Philo's loose views of inspiration cannot be declared irreconcilable with the acceptance of a fixed canon, unless it is first shown that he places others whom he thinks inspired on a level with the writers of Scripture. This he never does. And the sharp discrimination which he makes is evidenced by the fact that his recognition of sacred books is limited, as has been shown above, to the strict Hebrew canon. And the supreme authority accorded to it by Philo and his Jewish countrymen is apparent from his language, as reported by Eusebius,[1] " They have not changed so much as a single word in them. They would rather die a thousand deaths than detract anything from these laws and statutes."

Movers, p. 21 f., argues that all the books in the Septuagint must have been regarded as canonical by the Alexandrian Jews, and as they maintained a close connection with their brethren in Palestine in all religious matters, and derived their canon from them, these books must have been canonical likewise in Palestine, and were only excluded from the canon in both places at a later time, viz., the second century A.D., when the opinion became prevalent that inspiration had ceased after Malachi (p. 31 f.). This extraordinary opinion is sufficiently refuted by the proofs already given, that the canon, both in Palestine and Alexandria, coincided precisely with the books now found in the Hebrew Bible.

[1] De Prep. Evang., lib. viii., quoted by Cosin, p. 16.

Movers seems to have been the first to direct attention to certain expressions in the Talmud, from which he drew the inference that the limits of the canon were not finally settled until the second century A.D. Great stress has since been laid by critics upon these passages as showing that the canon, and particularly the third division of the canon, was long in an unsettled and fluctuating condition.

Two technical expressions are found in the passages in question. One is גָּנַז, *ganaz*, to withdraw from sacred use. This was applied to manuscripts of the sacred books which, on account of errors of transcription, were pronounced unfit for synagogue use; also to manuscripts which were old and worn out, and were, in consequence, buried in a spot called *Gheniza*, to protect them from profanation; also to portions of the sacred books which were not considered suitable for reading in the public worship of the synagogue. To *ganaz* a book is, accordingly, to forbid its use in the synagogue worship, which is practically equivalent to excluding it from the canon.

The other technical expression is to "defile the hands." "Books of Scripture were said to defile the hands. To say that a given book defiled the hands is to declare that it belongs to the sacred canon; to say that it does not defile the hands is to deny it a place in the canon. This singular dictum of the rabbis has been differently understood. The most natural explanation of it would seem to be that the sacred volume is so holy that no one must touch it without first washing his hands. Hands which are clean enough for ordinary purposes become unclean in the presence of this holy book, and thus the Scriptures defile the hands, causing them to be considered unclean, and needing to be cleansed before they can be suffered to come into contact with what is so pure." [1] The rabbis themselves give a different account of it. They explain it as an arbitrary regulation invented to guard the sacred books from injury. Lest the rolls containing them might be damaged by being suffered to lie near the grain of the first-fruits and other offerings, and thus be exposed to the danger of being gnawed by the mice which this grain would attract, it was enacted that these rolls would defile the heave-offerings, and would defile the hands of him who touched them, so that he could not handle those offerings. [2]

Questionings are said to have arisen respecting Ezekiel and Proverbs which were set at rest after prolonged investigation. It is mentioned that certain rabbis of the school of Shammai denied that Ecclesiastes defiled the hands, while those of the rival school of Hillel affirmed that it did. Others are spoken of as doubting whether the Song of Solomon defiled the hands, and a like doubt was expressed about Esther. But the inspiration of Esther was affirmed, and at a great assembly held at Jamnia, near the close of the first century A.D., [3] the seventy-two elders resolved that the Song of Solomon and Ecclesiastes do defile the hands. [4]

[1] Fürst, Kanon, p. 83.

[2] Herzfeld, Geschichte, III., p. 97; Delitzsch in Luth. Zeitschrift for 1854, p. 280, quotes from the Talmudic Tract, Sabbath, "Because they used to lay the heave-offering beside the book of the Law and thought: This is holy and that is holy. But when they saw that the books of the Law were thus exposed to the risk of injury, the Rabbis resolved that the Holy Scriptures should be regarded as unclean."

[3] Robertson Smith, p. 185, dates it cir. 90 A.D.; Delitzsch, ubi supra, p. 282, A.D. 118.

[4] Bloch, p. 152, insists that "defiling the hands" or "not defiling the hands" has nothing to do with the canonicity of the books to which these expressions are applied. He says: "It is decidedly an error if that prophylactic regulation that certain sacred books (preeminently those of Moses) cause Levitical defilement is put in relation

Robertson Smith, pp. 176 ff., alleges on this ground that only a certain portion of the Old Testament was fixed and incontestable among the Jews, and that the canonical authority of other parts was disputed and long stood in doubt. While there never has been any dispute of the canonicity of the Law, the Prophets, and three large Poetical books, which stand first in the Hagiographa, viz., the Psalms, Proverbs, and Job, the books which follow are a later addition, and some of the Jews themselves questioned whether certain of them, particularly the Song of Solomon, Ecclesiastes, and Esther belonged to the canon; and this strife was not finally concluded in their favor until nearly one hundred years after the beginning of the Christian era.[1]

In regard to these disputations it is to be observed,

1. That the question in every case was not whether a book should or should not be admitted to the canon, as though this had never before been decided; but whether a book, which had long before been received into the canon, was rightfully there or ought to be excluded from it.

to the collection of the canon or to the canonical character of a book. Besides Ecclesiastes and the Song of Solomon, there were other acknowledged canonical books to which that ordinance was not extended; and the Shammaites, the alleged opposers of Ecclesiastes, have, as can be shown, never doubted its canonical character." " It is declared (Kelim, xiv. 6) that those ordinances, according to which the Pentateuch and other sacred writings cause Levitical defilement, do not apply to the high-priest's copy of the Pentateuch, which was kept in the temple. Here we see clearly that the entire regulation stands in no relation to the canonical character of the books." He refers to his treatise on Ecclesiastes for a statement of the real reason of the order that certain books of Scripture produce Levitical defilement. This treatise I have not seen. Of course, if Bloch can establish his contention, this whole matter becomes irrelevant. It is here discussed on the assumption that the phrase has the meaning which scholars generally put upon it.

[1] Derenbourg, Histoire de la Palestine, pp. 295 ff., makes the number of antilegomena still greater.

2. The grounds of objection did not affect the authorship or genuineness of the books, but rest upon exceptions taken to the contents of the books themselves, implying a high and well-established standard of canonical fitness, to which every book included in the canon must be expected to conform. The Song of Solomon, considered as a mere song of worldly love, and Ecclesiastes in its commendation of worldly enjoyment, were thought to fall below this standard. Some of the objections are frivolous and trivial, and seem to have been made for the sake of refuting them by a display of subtlety. And none of them were of such a character as to lead to the omission of any of these books from the canon. When submitted to the assembly of elders the objections were overruled, and the books retained. And the Talmud in other passages abundantly testifies to the canonical authority of the disputed books. Instead of proving that the canon was still unsettled, these objections were directed against a canon already firmly established, and left it in the same condition in which they found it. The questionings of individual rabbis are of no account against the universal sentiment of the Jewish Church.[1]

[1] Strack, p. 429, speaks very decidedly on this point: " Seriously meant contradictions against the canon of the twenty-four sacred books were never raised in ancient Jewry; books once received were neither seriously contested, nor was any book, that is spoken of in the preceding discussion as not received, ever subsequently admitted, or attempts made to admit it. In all the Talmudic disputations the question was not of the reception of new books, nor of the enlargement of the canon, nor of the exclusion of a book on the ground of any critical doubts, but only that individual scholars adduced reasons taken from the contents for the exclusion of one book or another long since received, without in a single instance practical effect being given to these discussions. The debates often make the impression that the doubts were only raised in order to be contradicted; in other words, on the one hand as an exercise of acuteness, and on the other to demonstrate

3. These objections were not limited to what Robertson Smith regards as the disputed portion of the canon; but, such as they were, they were directed against what he considers the unquestioned portion as well, *e.g.*, against Proverbs and the Book of Ezekiel.

4. The idea of an unsettled canon in the first century of the Christian era is absolutely inadmissible in the

the authority of the sacred books as absolutely assured. There is no passage from which it follows that there ever was any wavering in the religious consciousness of the people as to the canonicity of any one of the twenty-four books."

Herzfeld, Geschichte, III., p. 97, says to the same purport: "The question was not of newly receiving books, but of exscinding those that had long been received for important reasons. . . . But I doubt whether a book already admitted to the canon was ever actually removed in consequence. When it is said, in Aboth R. Nathan, ch. i., that Proverbs, the Song of Solomon, and Ecclesiastes were actually made apocryphal, until the Great Synagogue explained what was strange in them and put an end to their exclusion, it may be affirmed that so recent an account deserves no faith, as opposed to those older ones which differ from it."

So, too, Buhl, Kanon und Text, p. 25 : " Such attacks upon books of the Bible do not exclude an earlier fixed canon, since the criticism of particular writings of the Old Testament were not altogether silenced after the Synod of Jamnia, nor even after the decision of the Mishnah. Further, the very attacks referred to, more carefully considered, actually presuppose a canon of Scripture. The question was not of the genuineness or age of the writings impugned, but only of doubts and scruples which were called forth by a definitely developed, dogmatic conception of Scripture; since from the notion of a strictly limited Scripture, sundered from all other literature, they felt entitled to institute certain demands of the harmonious unity and moral and religious purity of this Scripture. Josephus boasts in the passage above adduced that the sacred literature of the Jews did not consist, like that of other nations, of discordant and conflicting books. The very offence which was taken at that time at the writings in question, and which compelled the defenders of them to resort to all sorts of strange, forced interpretations, that were ultimately approved by all Jews, is the most convincing proof that they felt very strongly bound to take these accused books under their protection, which can only be properly explained on the aforesaid presupposition."

face of the explicit testimony of Josephus. However
the critics may try to persuade themselves that he was
mistaken in fixing the time of the completion of the
canon as far back as the reign of Artaxerxes Longimanus, he certainly knew in what esteem the sacred books
were held in his own day, and the convictions of his
countrymen in regard to them. And he could not possibly have said that nothing had been added to them or
taken from them, or altered in them, in all the time that
had elapsed since Artaxerxes, if the true limits of the
canon were still in doubt, or certain books had found a
place in it within a decennium.

Wildeboer claims that the number of books in the
K'thubhim were not fixed, nor the Old Testament canon
closed, till the middle of the second century, when, he
says (p. 146), "we may reckon that all scribes were
agreed upon the subject." And yet he adds (p. 150):
"The notices in the Gemara prove that the objections
were not forgotten. That they were still felt is shown
by Megilla (fol. 7a), where the objection against Esther
is brought up by R. Samuel, who lived in the third century A.D." If individual doubts prove an unsettled
canon, consistency would have required him to say that
it was not yet closed in the third century. But he substantially yields the whole case by the admission (p.
147) : "Josephus proves most clearly that the number
was virtually fixed about 100 A.D. Public opinion was
really already settled. But it awaited its sanction from
the schools." And (p. 46), "A general settled persuasion in regard to canonicity preceded the decision of
the schools. In the days of Josephus the schools still
had their doubts about certain books of the third division. But among the people there existed in his days
such a reverence for precisely the books which still constitute our canon (as the number given by Josephus

proves) that, 'if need be, they would gladly die for them.'" Such a universal conviction on the part of the mass of the people is not set aside by the questionings of a few individual doctors. "The decision of the schools" has not the power to make or unmake the canon, whether in the days of Josephus or in our own. And if the statement of Josephus proves anything, it proves that the canon was not only settled at the moment of his writing, but that it had been settled for a very long period before that.

It has further been represented that the books of Baruch and Ecclesiasticus are accorded canonical authority in certain passages of the Talmud. But this is an utter mistake. Strack, who is an authority in post-biblical Jewish literature, declares that not a single proof can be adduced from the entire range of Jewish writings, whether of Palestine or Babylonia, that Baruch was held in such high esteem. He also affirms that the like statement regarding Ecclesiasticus is unfounded. In a few instances this book seems to be cited with the same formulas that are used in quoting Holy Scripture, *e.g.*, with the phrase, "it is written." But in some of these passages it can be shown that the correct text reads, "it is written in the Book of Sirach" or Ecclesiasticus, which of course conveys no implication of canonicity, and the context is directly opposed to such an implication. In a very few other passages it would seem as though the citation were made from memory, and the similarity of its style to the canonical writings of Solomon had betrayed the writer into the mistake of supposing that the verse cited was from the Bible. But that this must have arisen from inadvertence is plain, since in no place in the Talmud or in any Jewish writer, ancient or modern, is Ecclesiasticus reckoned among the books of Scripture; on the contrary, it is over and over again expressly excluded from the canon.

This book of the son of Sirach, with its moral and religious tone, its apparent claim of inspiration (xxiv. 32–34, xxxiii. 16–18), and written in Hebrew, was excluded from the canon, as the critics aver, solely on account of its recent origin. And yet the Book of Daniel, which they confidently assert was written at a still later date, was nevertheless admitted to the canon with such unquestioning unanimity, that not a whisper of objection of any sort is made to it in any Jewish writing, though doubts were expressed respecting other books of acknowledged antiquity. This has occasioned them much perplexity. They say it is because it was attributed to Daniel, though really written in the time of the Maccabees. But how such an origin could have been unhesitatingly ascribed by the contemporary generation to a book produced in their own time, and such implicit faith reposed in its unaccredited contents, is a puzzle.

The following passages from the Talmud are adduced as indicating doubts respecting the canonicity of certain books of the Old Testament:

" Remember that man for good, Hananiah, son of Hezekiah, by name [a younger contemporary of Hillel at the time of the birth of Christ], since but for him the Book of Ezekiel would have been withdrawn (ganaz), because its words contradict the words of the law. What did he do? They brought up to him 300 measures of oil, and he sat in an upper room and explained them." Sabbath 13b, Hagiga 13a, Menahoth 45a (Fürst, Kanon, p. 24).

" The wise men desired to withdraw (ganaz) the Book of Ecclesiastes because its language was often self-contradictory and contradicted the utterances of David. Why did they not withdraw it? Because the beginning and the end of it consist of words of the law." Sabbath 30b (after Ryle, pp. 195, 197).

" Some desired also to withdraw (ganaz) the Book of Proverbs, because it contained internal contradictions (e.g., xxvi. 4, 5), but the attempt was abandoned because the wise men declared, ' We have examined more deeply into the Book of Ecclesiastes, and have discovered the solution of the difficulty; here also we wish to inquire more deeply." Sabbath 30b (Ryle, p. 194 f.).

" At first they said that Proverbs, Canticles, and Ecclesiastes are apocryphal (genuzim). They said they were parabolic writings and not of the Hagiographa . . . till the men of the Great Synagogue came and explained them." Aboth of R. Nathan, c. i. (Robertson Smith, p. 181.)

" All the Holy Scriptures defile the hands; the Song of Solomon and Ecclesiastes defile the hands. R. Judah says, The Song of Solomon defiles the hands, and Ecclesiastes is disputed. R. Jose says, Ecclesiastes does not defile the hands, and the Song of Solomon is disputed. R. Simon says, Ecclesiastes belongs to the light things of the School of Shammai, and the heavy things of the school of Hillel [*i.e.*, the usually rigorous school of Shammai here departs from the accepted view that Ecclesiastes defiles the hands, while that of Hillel adheres to it]. R. Simeon, son of Azzai says, I received it as a tradition from the seventy-two elders on the day when they enthroned R. Eliezer, son of Azariah [as President of the Beth Din at Jamnia, which became the seat of the heads of the Scribes after the fall of Jerusalem], that the Song of Solomon and Ecclesiastes defile the hands. R. Akiba said, Silence and Peace ! No one in Israel has ever doubted that the Song of Solomon defiles the hands. For no day in the history of the world is worth the day when the Song of Solomon was given to Israel. For all the Hagiographa are holy, but the Song of Solomon is a holy of holies. If there has been any dispute, it referred only to Ecclesiastes. . . . So they disputed, and so they decided." Yadaim, iii. 5 (Robertson Smith, p. 186).

" Ecclesiastes does not defile the hands according to the school of Shammai, but does so according to the school of Hillel." Eduyoth, v. 3 (ibid., p. 186).

" According to R. Judah, Samuel said : Esther does not defile the hands. Are we then to say that, in the opinion of Samuel, Esther was not spoken under the influence of the Holy Spirit. It was spoken to be read, and was not spoken to be written. . . . R. Simeon says : Ruth, Song of Solomon and Esther defile the hands. In opposition to Simeon, Samuel agrees with Joshua that Esther was only intended to be read, not to be written. According to a Baraitha, R. Simeon ben Manasya said : Ecclesiastes does not defile the hands, because it contains Solomon's own wisdom. He was answered : Is Ecclesiastes the only thing that Solomon spake? Does not the Scripture say that he spake three thousand proverbs (1 Kin. iv. 32)? Yet this Solomon says

(Prov. **xxx**. 6): Add not to his words. What is the force of this proof? You might think: He spake much; if he wished, it was written down; if he wished, it was not written down. But this idea is contradicted by Add not to his words." [The meaning is, Solomon made no addition to the words of God. Ecclesiastes, therefore, is not Solomon's own wisdom, which might or might not be written, as he pleased, but a divine book.] Megilla, i. 7a. (Delitzsch, ibid., p. 283.)

Delitzsch understands this obscure passage to mean that, while Esther was inspired, it was intended only to be orally preserved, and not committed to writing, and consequently did not defile the hands. According to Fürst, p. 57, though it was admitted to have been written under the influence of the Holy Spirit, the contention was that it should only be regarded as history, and not as belonging to the K'thubhim, until finally the wise approved of its reception.

The Jerusalem Talmud says, Megilloth, fol. 70, 74, that 85 elders, among whom were more than 30 prophets, ridiculed the introduction of the feast of Purim by Esther and Mordecai as an innovation upon the law. Bleek, Einleitung, p. 404.

Some expressions of Jerome are also appealed to as reflecting Jewish disputes respecting canonical books.

"The beginning and end of Ezekiel are involved in obscurities, and among the Hebrews these parts, and the exordium of Genesis, must not be read by a man under thirty." Epistle to Paulinus (from Robertson Smith, p. 176).

"The Hebrews say, when it seemed as though this book should be obliterated along with other writings of Solomon which are antiquated and have not been kept in memory, because it asserts that the creatures of God are vanity, and that all amounts to nothing, and prefers eating and drinking and transient pleasures to all besides; on account of this one paragraph it was deservedly authorized to be put in the number of divine books, because it concluded the whole disputation and the entire account in this summing up, as it were, and said the end of the discourses was one most suitable to be heard and had nothing difficult in it, to wit, that we should fear God and keep his commandments." Comment on Ecclesiastes, xii. 13, 14 (from Ryle, p. 197).

THE CANON OF CHRIST AND HIS APOSTLES

THE history of the formation and the collection of the canon among the Jews has now been traced, and the extent of the canon received by them has been considered. The next point to be considered is, What books were recognized as belonging to the Old Testament by the Lord Jesus Christ and the inspired writers of the New Testament? They have not left us a list of these books, but they have clearly indicated their mind in this matter, so that we need be under no mistake as to their meaning. They give their infallible and authoritative sanction to the canon as it existed among the Jews. This is done both negatively and positively. They sanction the integrity of the Scriptures of the Jews negatively, in that they never charge them with mutilating or corrupting the word of God. Our Lord repeatedly rebukes them for making void the word of God by their traditions. At various times he corrects their false glosses and erroneous interpretations of Scripture. But while censuring them for this, he could not have passed it over in silence, if they had been guilty of excluding whole books from the canon which properly belonged there, or inserting that which was not really inspired of God.

The positive sanction which they give to the Jewish canon is afforded:

1. By express statements, as in Rom. iii. 2, "Unto them [the Jews] were committed the oracles of God," or

as rendered in the R. V., "They were intrusted with the oracles of God." 2 Tim. iii. 16, "All Scripture [the body of writings so called by the Jews] is given by inspiration of God," or more emphatically still in the R. V., "Every Scripture inspired of God," *i.e.*, every part of that collection of writings known as Scripture is here not merely affirmed but assumed to be inspired of God, and this assumption is made the basis of the declaration as to its profitable character. The spiritual profit derived from it is not here made the test of inspiration, but its acknowledged inspiration is the credential which gives assurance that the man of God will be by it furnished completely unto every good work.

2. By general references to the sacred books by their familiar designations, either those which describe them as a whole, as the Scriptures, Mat. xxii. 29, "Ye do err, not knowing the Scriptures," John v. 39, "Search the Scriptures," x. 35, "The Scripture cannot be broken," Luke xxiv. 45, Acts xvii. 11, Rom. iv. 3, x. 11; Holy Scriptures, Rom. i. 2, 2 Tim. iii. 15; or which speak of them under their commonly recognized divisions, as the law and the prophets, Mat. v. 17, vii. 12, xi. 13, xxii. 40, Luke xvi. 16, 29, 31, John i. 45, Acts xxiv. 14, xxviii. 23, Rom. iii. 21, these prominent portions being put for the whole, or "prophets" being used in a wide sense so as to embrace all the inspired writers after Moses, cf. Heb. i. 1; or with allusion to the threefold division of the canon, Luke xxiv. 44, "the law of Moses, and the prophets, and the Psalms." In this last passage "the Psalms" has sometimes been understood as denoting the entire Hagiographa, of which it is the first and leading book. But it is doubtless used, in its strict and proper sense, to designate the book so called, which is here singled out from the rest of the third division of the canon as that which specially testifies of Christ.

All the books without exception are, however, spoken of in the same connection, verse 27, " And beginning from Moses and from all the prophets, he interpreted to them in all the Scriptures the things concerning himself."

3. By the abundant citation of passages from the Old Testament as the word of God, as the language of the Holy Ghost, or as the utterance of inspired men. Nearly every book in the Old Testament is thus quoted. With the exception of Ezra, Nehemiah, Esther, Ecclesiastes, and the Song of Solomon, they are all quoted in the New Testament.[1]

Every such quotation sanctions, of course, the canonicity of the book that is thus cited. If a few books are not quoted, this does not justify the suspicion that they were excluded from the canon; it is simply because the inspired writers of the New Testament had no occasion to make citations from them. Their citations are made as appropriate passages offer themselves for the illustration or enforcement of their particular theme, with no preconceived purpose of making use in this manner of every book which they esteemed canonical. And it may be fairly claimed that their citations are of such a nature as to extend their sanction not only over the books which are explicitly quoted, but over the entire collection in which they are found. They take the collection of sacred books commonly received among the Jews, and quote from it freely, as they find occasion.

[1] Three of the briefest of the Minor Prophets, Obadiah, Nahum, and Zephaniah are not separately quoted; these are not to be reckoned exceptions, however, as the Twelve were anciently regarded as one book; and the canonicity of the others being established, that of these follows of course. It has been claimed that Eccles. vii. 20 is cited in Rom. iii. 10; Eccles. v. 14 in 1 Tim. vi. 7; Esth. ix. 22 in Rev. xi. 10, and Solomon's Song v. 2 in Rev. iii. 20. If these allusions are allowed, the number of books not cited will be correspondingly reduced.

And every passage which they adduce is put forth as possessing divine authority. They could in no way more significantly show that they regarded the entire collection, with all that it contained, as the inspired word of God.

To those who reverently accept the authority of Christ and his apostles, the sanction thus given to the canon of the Jews is the highest possible proof of its correctness.[1] It contains just those books which were designed of God to form the rule of faith and life for the Jewish Church, and to be transmitted by them to the Church of all time. In reply to this, however, it has been said that the writers of the New Testament

---

[1] Moses Stuart, the father of Hebrew learning in this country, says, Old Testament Canon, p. 316 : " While I am not fond of applying harsh and ungrateful epithets to any man or body of men whatever, I know not how to call the denying or the designed evading of the authority or the decision of Christ and of his apostles respecting the books of the Old Testament, anything less than unbelief." Wildeboer allows himself to use the following most extraordinary language, p. 153 : " It was impossible that Jesus should acknowledge the Old Testament Canon as such, although in His days about the same books were, no doubt, accounted to belong to the Holy Scriptures as are found in our own Old Testament. But what a misconception of Jesus' person and teaching comes out in the idea that the Saviour felt himself bound to a Canon ! . . . Did he need for this the sanction of synagogue and scribes? . . . The notion that *the* Prophet, the Revelation of God by pre-eminence, deemed Himself bound by a Canon can only arise in a heart so ignorant of the whole nature of scientific criticism, and, therefore, so afraid of it, that it will rather admit a gross inconsistency in its conception of the Saviour than let go its cherished tradition." Christ's recognition of the Jewish canon as the unadulterated word of God, and his frequently repeated appeal to it as such, is not subjecting himself to the authority of the synagogue and the scribes. It is, on the contrary, his affirmation on his own independent authority that, in this particular, they have made no mistake. The imputation of such a view to those who cannot accept the groundless conclusions of the critics respecting the formation of the canon, is a gross and gratuitous misrepresentation.

made use of the Septuagint version in quoting from the Old Testament, and hence must be regarded as sanctioning the canonicity of all the books which that version contained.

1. In making use of the Septuagint, as the New Testament writers frequently do, they by no means sanction its inaccuracies of text or of translation, nor the spurious additions made to the canon, even if it be admitted that the apocryphal books were then already incorporated with this version, of which there is no certain proof.[1] They employ its familiar words, so far as they are adapted to the purpose which they have in view, without pedantically correcting unessential departures from the Hebrew original which do not affect their argument or their line of remark. In all this they are responsible only for the inherent truthfulness of each passage in the form which they actually adopt.

2. The apostles were not liable to be misunderstood in this matter. Unless they made explicit declarations to the contrary, they would as a matter of course be regarded as accepting the canon currently received among the Jews. And, as has already been shown, the Jews admitted just those books to be canonical which are now found in the Hebrew Bible, and no others.

3. While the New Testament writers quote freely and abundantly from the canonical books, they never quote from any of the Apocrypha, much less do they ascribe to them inspiration or canonicity. Attempts have indeed been made to point out quotations from the Apocrypha, but without success, as is evident from the detailed examination of the passages in question by

---

[1] "It must be remembered that scarcely anyone in those days possessed a complete collection of the Holy Scriptures; most of the synagogues even were not so rich. And if anyone had them all, *the rolls were all separate.*" Wildeboer, p. 50.

Bishop Cosin [1] and Dr. Thornwell.[2] In every instance of alleged citation it appears upon inspection, either (1) that the resemblance is not so close as to show that one passage has borrowed from the other, or to preclude the idea that both have been independently conceived, particularly if the thought expressed is some ordinary truth of biblical faith or morals. Or else (2) the apocryphal passage is itself conformed to one in the canonical books of the Old Testament; and it is the latter, not the former, which the New Testament writer had in mind.

Bleek, in his elaborate article written to justify the retention of the Apocrypha as an appendix to the Old Testament,[3] freely admits that there are no citations, properly speaking, of these books in the New Testament, but claims (p. 336) that "most of the New Testament writings exhibit more or less certain traces of an acquaintance with our Apocrypha, and reminiscences from them," and (p. 349) " unmistakable allusions to their contents, and manifest traces of their influence on the conceptions, mode of expression and language of the New Testament writers." Of this he admits that there is no " convincing proof," only a high degree of " probability." The passages to which he refers as illustrative of his position contain some coincidences in thought and expression, *e.g.*, James i. 19, Ecclus v. 11; Rom. ix.

---

[1] Scholastical History of the Canon, pp. 23–28. The following are alleged as parallels : Wisd. ix. 13, Rom. xi. 34 (Isa. xl. 13) ; Wisd. vii. 26, Heb. i. 3; Wisd. iv. 10, Heb. xi. 5 (Gen. v. 24); Wisd. vi. 3, Rom. xiii. 1 (Prov. viii. 15, 16); Wisd. vi. 7, Rom. ii. 11 (Deut. x. 17); Ecclus. xiv. 17, James i. 10, 1 Pet. i. 24 (Isa. xl. 6, 7); Tobit iv. 7, Luke xi. 41; Tob. iv. 12, 1 Thess. iv. 3; Tob. iv. 15, Mat. vii. 12; Baruch iv. 7, 1 Cor. x. 20 (Deut. xxxii. 17); and others like them.

[2] Arguments of Romanists Discussed and Refuted, pp. 162-174.

[3] Ueber die Stellung der Apokryphen des alten Testamentes im Christlichen Kanon, in the Studien und Kritiken for 1853, pp. 267–354.

21, Wisdom xv. 7 (cf. Jer. xviii. 6); Eph. vi. 13–17, Wisd. v. 17–20 ; John vi. 35, Ecclus. xxiv. 21, which may be purely accidental, or may betray an acquaintance with these writings that has consciously or unconsciously affected the form of statement. But if all for which Bleek contends were conceded, it would amount to nothing more than that the sacred writers were aware of the existence of some of the apocryphal books and approved certain sentiments expressed in them. And this is very far from ascribing to them divine authority or canonical standing. Stier, who goes far beyond Bleek in tracing a supposed connection between the New Testament writers and the Apocrypha, nevertheless remarks, " It is unconditionally limited to bare allusion, and never passes over to actual citation." [1]

In Heb. xi. 35b, " Others were tortured, not accepting their deliverance ; that they might obtain a better resurrection," there is prominent though not exclusive reference to the martyrdom of Eleazar and the mother with her seven sons, of which an account is given in 2 Macc. vi. 18–vii. 42. This is a recognition of the historical truth of the facts thus referred to, but does not imply the canonicity of the book in which they are recorded.

" They were sawn asunder " (ver. 37), may allude in part at least to the martyrdom of Isaiah, if he was indeed put to death in this manner by Manasseh, agreeably to Jewish tradition. But the sacred writer surely does not canonize hereby any fabulous account of the transaction.

It is further claimed that there are several direct quotations from Pseudepigrapha in the New Testament, made in the same manner as those which are taken from the canonical books. The most noted of these is

---

[1] Quoted by Oehler, Herzog Encyk., VII., p. 257.

Jude vs. 14, 15. " And to these also Enoch, the seventh from Adam, prophesied, saying, Behold, the Lord came with ten thousands of his holy ones to execute judgment upon all, and to convict all the ungodly of all their works of ungodliness which they have ungodly wrought, and of all the hard things which ungodly sinners have spoken against him." This appears to be taken from the Book of Enoch, ch. ii. It is to be observed, however, that this is, after all, nothing more than a natural inference from what is recorded of Enoch in the Book of Genesis. A man who walked with God and was specially favored by him, in the midst of abounding wickedness could not do otherwise than rebuke his contemporaries for their ungodliness, and warn them of the coming judgment of a holy God. In accepting this legitimate conclusion from the sacred narrative, Jude gives no sanction to the fabulous contents of the book whose language he has in this single instance seen fit to adopt ; much less does he, as Bleek affirms, recognize it " as a genuine production and an authentic source for divine revelation." He does not do this any more than the Apostle Paul in citing a single sentence from each of the Greek poets, Aratus, Menander, and Epimenides, thereby endorses all that they have written, or attributes to them any sacred character.

Clement of Alexandria and Origen found in Jude ver. 9, " Michael, the archangel, when contending with the devil he disputed about the body of Moses, durst not bring against him a railing judgment, but said The Lord rebuke thee," a quotation from the Assumption of Moses. This suggestion cannot be verified, as the book is not now in existence, and its origin is unknown. But Jude's language finds a ready explanation in Zech. iii. 1, 2, where the angel of the Lord, contending with Satan on behalf of the people (figuratively styled the body of

Moses, after the analogy of the Church as the body of Christ), says to him, The Lord rebuke thee.

James iv. 6 in the A. V. reads, "Do ye think that the Scripture saith in vain, The spirit that dwelleth in us lusteth to envy?" This rendering has given rise to the conjecture, on the one hand, that the second clause of the verse gives the substance of some passage in the Old Testament, like Gen. vi. 5, viii. 21; Num. xi. 4, 29, or Prov. xxi. 10, and, on the other, that it is borrowed from some writing now lost and otherwise unknown. But when the passage is correctly rendered, as in the R. V. (see marg.), the need of these conjectures disappears: "Or think ye that the Scripture speaketh in vain? That Spirit, which he made to dwell in us, yearneth *for us* even unto jealous envy." The second clause of the verse is the Apostle James' own language, not a citation from some earlier Scripture. And his meaning is, that the jealous longing which God's Spirit has for the undivided love of men shows it to be no vain or unmeaning utterance when the Scriptures represent the love of the world as incompatible with the love of God.

1 Cor. ii. 9, "As it is written, Things which eye saw not, and ear heard not, and which entered not into the heart of man, whatsoever things God prepared for them that love him," is a slightly modified citation of Isa. lxiv. 4, "Men have not heard, nor perceived by the ear, neither hath the eye seen, a God beside thee who worketh for him that waiteth for him." It was so understood by Jerome, and before him by Clement of Rome, who, in his Epistle to the Corinthians, repeats these words of Paul, only bringing them into closer accord with Isaiah by substituting "them that wait for him" for "them that love him." There is no occasion, therefore, for Origen's conjecture, repeated by some in

modern times, that it is borrowed from the lost Apocalypse of Elias.

Eph. v. 14, " Wherefore he saith, Awake, thou that sleepest, and arise from the dead, and Christ shall shine upon thee," is simply a paraphrase of Isa. lii. 1, " Awake, awake, O Zion," combined with lx. 1, " Arise, shine, for thy light is come, and the glory of the Lord is risen upon thee." The call "awake" is impliedly addressed to a sleeper, and " arise " to one that is dead, and the shining comes from the light and glory of the Lord. It is just such an adaptation as is made of Ps. lxviii. 18 in iv. 8 of the same Epistle, where "ascending on high" is said to imply previous "descent into the lower parts of the earth." It is of small moment whether this paraphrase of Isaiah was made by the apostle himself, or, as some have supposed, by an early Christian poet, whose language Paul borrows. In either case there is no occasion for the conjecture of Epiphanius, and those who have followed him in modern times, that it is taken from the lost Apocalypse of Elias.

John vii. 38, " He that believeth on me, as the Scripture hath said, out of his belly shall flow rivers of living water." These precise words are not found elsewhere. The thought expressed is the familiar biblical truth that the true believer shall be blessed and be a blessing. And the emblem employed to represent this blessing and its ever-widening influence, that of perennial streams of living water, is one of frequent occurrence in the Old Testament. In Isa. lviii. 11, " Thou shalt be like a watered garden, and like a spring of water, whose waters fail not," the same thought and emblem are combined with only a change in the form of expression, cf. Isa. xliv. 3; Zech. xiv. 8. It has been conjectured that the Saviour borrowed these words from some writing otherwise unknown, which he here dignifies by the name of "Scripture." But the conjecture has no confirmation from any quarter whatever. There is no intimation from any source that such a writing ever existed. And the conjecture is wholly uncalled for, since the Saviour's language can be adequately explained without it.

Luke xi. 49, "Therefore, also, said the wisdom of God, I will send unto them prophets and apostles ; and some of them they shall kill and persecute." What God in his wisdom is here said to have resolved to do to the Jewish people is in the parallel passage (Mat. xxiii. 34) introduced as the language of Christ himself to his immediate hearers and the people of his time. There is no inconsistency between these statements. What God had purposed and done in the past, and was continuing to do in the present, is identical with what Christ was now actually doing. He was in this simply putting into effect the will of his Father. The reference in Luke is not to some particular passage in which these precise words occur, but to the whole course of God's dealings with this people, in which his purpose in this matter was exhibited. The assumption that Christ quotes these words from some writing now lost is altogether groundless.

In 2 Tim. iii. 8, the magicians of Egypt who withstood Moses are called "Jannes and Jambres." Whether these names were actually borne by them or not, these were their familiar designations among the Jews, as appears from the use made of them in the Targum of Jonathan. Paul employs these names commonly given to them as sufficient to identify the persons to whom he referred. There is no necessity, therefore, to suppose that he is here quoting "a lost book on the times of Moses."

Whatever explanation be adopted of the occurrence of "Jeremiah," in Mat. xxvii. 9, where "Zechariah" might have been expected, there is no need of resorting for a solution to Jerome's statement in his commentary on this passage, "Legi nuper in quodam Hebraico volumine, quod Nazarenæ sectæ mihi Hebræus obtulit, Jeremiæ apocryphum, in quo hæc ad verbum scripta reperi." The probability is that this passage was inserted in the apocryphal Jeremiah from the Gospel of Matthew. There is not the slightest reason for believing that the evangelist borrowed it from this source, of whose origin and history nothing is known.

From this review of the whole case, it will appear with how little reason Wildeboer asserts (p. 51), "A number of reminiscences and quotations from apocryphal writings prove very certainly that the New Testament writers recognized no canon of the Old Testament agreeing with ours." And (p. 53), "Many passages from apocryphal writings were present to the mind of the N. T. authors, which they often accorded equal weight with texts from the O. T. The apocrypha in question are not even those of the LXX.; for precisely in the actual quotations writings are used which are not found in the manuscripts of the LXX. It is manifest from this that most of the N. T. writers gave to the notion of 'Sacred Scripture' an even wider range than most of the Alexandrians." And (p. 56), "All the facts are explained by the hypothesis that in Jesus' days the competent authorities had not yet defined the canon; that only the Law and the Prophets enjoyed undisputed authority; that beside the Psalms, Daniel, and other books of the Kethubhim, many apocryphal writings also were freely read; but that over against this the schools were beginning to restrict and regulate their use. To this authority of the schools the Lord and his disciples would readily submit, and, if questioned, would have given an answer not very different from the later Jewish enumeration."

It has been shown that our Lord and the writers of the New Testament recognize the divine authority of the books esteemed sacred by the Jews abundantly and explicitly. They appeal to them as the word of God and the standard of truth and duty, as they never do to any other writings whatever. It may be that their language exhibits acquaintance with the Apocrypha, but they never quote them, nor make any such use of them as implies that they regarded them as divinely authoritative, or placed them in this respect on a level with the books of the Old Testament. The Epistle to the Hebrews refers to martyrdoms related in Maccabees, and adds them to a series of illustrations of the power of faith drawn from the Scriptures ; but it does not on this account rank Maccabees with the Scriptures. Historical facts may be attested by profane as well as by sacred sources. Jude, without vouching either for the genuineness or the divine authority of the Book of Enoch, makes use of its language to state a truth which may be plainly inferred from the record in Genesis. Other quotations are alleged from Pseudepigrapha, but it has been shown by an examination of each case in particular that there is not the slightest evidence on which to base such an assertion. Wildeboer indeed says (p. 51), "The fact that the N. T. writers quote from apocryphal books [it is plain from the connection that this term is here used in the sense of pseudepigraphical] can only be denied by dogmatic prejudice." But he forgets that what he is pleased to call "dogmatic prejudice," viz., a firm persuasion that the books of the Old Testament were specifically different from other Jewish writings, was shared by the Jews generally and by the New Testament writers as well; so that the absence of such a "dogmatic prejudice" cannot be essential to an unbiassed and sympathetic judgment of matters in which they are concerned. The submission of "the Lord and his disciples" "to the authority of the schools," which he here so naïvely asserts, is repelled with a display of pious fervor and holy indignation on pp. 153 f., where he falsely imputes it to those who are not content to follow the critics blindly in their baseless theories respecting the canon. See p. 144, note.

It is further urged that the limits of the canon were not yet definitely fixed in the time of our Lord, and that consequently his recognition of the acknowledged Jewish Scriptures cannot cover books which were then in dispute. Thus Robertson Smith (p. 187): "It is matter of fact that the position of several books was still subject of controversy in the apostolic age, and was not finally determined till after the fall of the Temple and the Jewish state. Before that date the Hagiographa did not form a closed collection, with an undisputed list of contents, and therefore the general testimony of Christ and the apostles to the Old Testament Scriptures cannot be used as certainly including books like Esther, Canticles, and Ecclesiastes, which were still disputed among the orthodox Jews in the apostolic age, and to which the New Testament never makes reference." But the Talmudic disputations here referred to do not disprove the existence of a definitely determined canon of long standing. They are the expression of individual doubts concerning particular books, based on a wrong view of their contents as inconsistent with the position accorded to them, and which were corrected by giving them a proper interpretation. They are of no more weight, accordingly, than like doubts, on similar grounds, which have been entertained in modern times. Nothing that

has been advanced to the contrary can annul the
evident fact that Christ and his apostles did give their
attestation to the canon commonly received among the
Jews. They distinguished, indeed, between the temporary form and the enduring substance of the Old
Testament. It was an inchoate revelation, and, as such,
had the imperfection which attaches to an unfinished
structure. There was much in it which was designed
to answer a transient purpose, and when that purpose
was accomplished the obligation ceased, Acts xv. 24;
Gal. iii. 24, 25. Some things were tolerated for a sea-
son because their "hardness of heart" unfitted the
people to receive anything better, Mat. xix. 8. Some
things were justifiable in saints of the former dispensation which were not to be imitated by the disciples of
Christ, with the fuller disclosures made to them of the
love and grace of God and the true spirit of the Gospel,
Luke ix. 54–56. The teachings of the Old Testament
were feeble and elementary, as compared with the more
advanced lessons of the New, Gal. iv. 9; Heb. x. 1.
Nevertheless, the Old Testament was the word of God
for the time then present. It was divinely adapted to
its special end of preparing the way for the coming and
the work of Christ. It was the foundation upon which
the Gospel was built, and was precisely fitted for the
superstructure to be erected upon it. Christ himself
said, "Think not that I came to destroy the law or the
prophets; I came not to destroy, but to fulfil. For
verily I say unto you, Till heaven and earth pass away,
one jot or tittle shall in no wise pass from the law till all
things be accomplished," Mat. v. 17, 18. The Apostle
Paul declares of himself that he "believed all things
which are according to the law and which are written in
the prophets," Acts xxiv. 14, and that he " said nothing
but what the prophets and Moses did say should come,"

xxvi. 22.   And he was careful to show that the doctrines
upon which he insisted were "witnessed by the law and
the prophets," Rom. iii. 21.   In its true intent and the
real essence of its teaching the Old Testament is of per-
petual validity.   Its temporary institutions are no longer
binding.   But the types and prophecies of the coming
Saviour still point to him as unerringly as ever.   The
elementary lessons of the early time have been supple-
mented by later and higher instructions, but are not
superseded by them.   The partial and the relative still
maintains its place, and fits into the absolute and the
perfect which has since been revealed.   Truth imperfectly disclosed is still true to the full extent to which
it goes, and is not annulled but absorbed when the full
truth is made known.   This is a necessary incident to
any course of instruction or training which is wisely
adapted to the growing capacities of the pupil.   The
Old Testament had its peculiar mission to the chosen
people before Christ came.   It has its mission still as
"living oracles" of God, Acts vii. 38, to all the world
through all time.

X

THE CANON OF THE CHRISTIAN CHURCH

THE canon of the Old Testament sanctioned by the Lord Jesus and his apostles must, beyond all doubt or question, be accepted as the true one by those who acknowledge their divine authority. Even Bellarmin[1] acknowledges that no books are canonical but those which the apostles approved and delivered to the Church.

A question here arises between Roman Catholics and Protestants as to the true extent of the Christian canon. The former contend that in addition to those which are contained in the Hebrew Bible, there are seven books and parts of two others which rightfully have a place in the canon of the Church. The books in dispute, commonly denominated the Apocrypha, are Tobit, Judith, Wisdom, Ecclesiasticus or Sirach, Baruch, 1st and 2d Maccabees, together with certain chapters added to Esther and Daniel in the Greek and Latin Bibles, which are not in the Hebrew.[2]

---

[1] De Verbo Dei, I., 20. Other Romanist authorities, however, have admitted that the apocryphal books have no express New Testament sanction. Thus Catherinus, one of the leading spirits in the Council of Trent, in his Opusc. de Script. Canonicis, says, "There are many books of the Old Testament, so called, and which are truly regarded as such, of which no testimony exists, as is evident enough, that they were approved by the apostles." And Stapleton, De Autorit. S. Script., II., 4, 14, "Wisdom, Ecclesiasticus, Tobit, Judith, and other books of the Old Testament were not confirmed in the times of the Apostles." Quoted by Cosin, p. 23.

[2] The Apocrypha of the English Bible contains, in addition, 1st and

It has been claimed that the apostolic sanction of these books must be presumed, inasmuch as they were accepted as the inspired word of God by the Christian Church, which would not have been the case unless by the direction and authority of the apostles. This brings us to inquire into the history of the canon in the Christian Church, and we shall find there, too, when the evidence is properly sifted and correctly explained, that the same books, and no others, were received as in the proper sense inspired and authoritative which had been accepted by the Jews and acknowledged by our Lord and his apostles. But if it were otherwise, this should not disturb our conclusion already reached. If it should prove to be the case that the Church had fallen into error with regard to the canon, as it has done in regard to other matters, its departures from the infallible and authoritative teaching of our Lord and his apostles would be no more binding in one case than in the other.

Before entering upon the inquiry into the belief and practice of the Christian Church in this matter, it will be necessary to say a few words respecting the meaning of the terms " canonical " and " apocryphal," which are constantly met with in the discussion of this subject. These words are used by Christian writers of the early ages in different senses; and it is important to know this in order to understand their meaning correctly.

" Canonical books " in ordinary usage then, as now, denoted books inspired of God, which were given to the Church as her rule of faith and life. But sometimes books were called " canonical " in a looser or wider sense, including together with the inspired books others which were denominated " ecclesiastical," because approved by the Church as useful and profitable religious

2d Esdras (= 3d and 4th Esdras of the Vulgate) and the Prayer of Manasseh, which are not accounted canonical by Romanists.

books, and commended to Christian people. In the former sense, the term "canonical" stands opposed to all uninspired productions. In the latter sense it includes certain books which were confessedly uninspired, and not properly speaking authoritative, but stands opposed to such as were pernicious and heretical. When cases occur in which the word is used in this latter sense, the proof will be furnished that such is actually the meaning intended.

Gieseler[1] instituted a careful inquiry into the meaning of "apocryphal" in the early Church, the result of which Bleek[2] sums up as follows: "Originally this designation seems not to have been used in a bad sense, and to have been opposed not to canonical, but to open or public, in reference to such writings as were assumed or asserted to have been preserved and perpetuated from early times by the way of secret transmission. The word appears to have been especially in use in this sense among the Gnostics for writings on which they chiefly relied for their doctrine, and which they attributed to distinguished men of former ages. So Clement of Alexandria says ('Strom.,' i. 15, 60) that the adherents of Prodicus boasted that they possessed apocryphal books of Zoroaster. But the greater the stress which the heretics laid upon these writings, the more they were suspected for this very reason by the teachers of the orthodox Church. They regarded them without hesitation—and in general, correctly—as late, counterfeit, patched-up productions of heretical contents, so that with them the notion of counterfeit was naturally associated with apocryphal. Thus Irenæus ('Adv. Hær.' i. 20), 'apocryphal and spurious writings.' Apostolical, Constitutions (vi. 16), 'Apocryphal books of Moses, and

---

[1] Was heisst apokryphisch ? in the Studien und Kritiken for 1829.
[2] Studien und Kritiken for 1853, pp. 267 ff.

Enoch, and Adam, Isaiah and David and Elijah and the three patriarchs, destructive and hostile to the truth.' In the first centuries this designation is never used in reference to those writings, or any of them, which we understand by the Apocrypha of the Old Testament. Hence these books, such as Wisdom, Ecclesiasticus, etc., are expressly distinguished both by Athanasius and by Ruffin from the canonical books of the Old Testament, but quite as expressly from apocryphal writings, and treated as a middle class—in Athanasius, 'books that are read;' in Ruffin, 'ecclesiastical books.'

"It is different with Jerome, who embraces under Apocrypha all those writings which, by their title or by partial recognition in the Church, make a claim to be put on a par with the canonical books, to which they are not rightfully entitled; and he does this irrespective of the contents of these writings, whether they are wholly objectionable or at least partially to be recommended for reading. Thus, he says, whatever is additional to these books translated from the Hebrew is to be placed among the Apocrypha."

Of the various ways by which the early Church renders its testimony to the canon of the Old Testament, the most explicit and satisfactory is the catalogues of the sacred books. Several of these catalogues have been preserved from individual writers of eminence and from councils; the latter have the advantage of being the joint testimony of considerable numbers, representing an entire province, or a still larger district of country.

The oldest catalogue of the books of the Old Testament, now extant, is that of Melito,[1] Bishop of Sardis (after A.D. 171), and this is the only catalogue dating from the second century. Melito informs us that he

---

[1] Preserved by Eusebius in his Ecclesiastical History, IV., 26.

had travelled into Judea, and made diligent inquiries there in order to arrive at certainty upon the subject. His list of books is the following : " Five of Moses, Genesis, Exodus, Leviticus, Numbers, Deuteronomy ; Joshua, Judges, Ruth, four of Kingdoms,[1] two of Chronicles, Psalms of David, Proverbs of Solomon, which is also Wisdom, Ecclesiastes, Song of Songs, Job ; the Prophets, Isaiah, Jeremiah, the Twelve in one book, Daniel, Ezekiel, Ezra." After the Proverbs of Solomon occur the words ἡ καὶ σοφία, from which the attempt has been made to draw an argument for the apocryphal Book of Wisdom. But the words will bear no other translation than " the Proverbs of Solomon, which is also Wisdom," i.e., this is another name given to the Book of Proverbs. Lamentations does not occur in this list, as that was reckoned a part of Jeremiah. Nehemiah also is not separately mentioned, as it was included in Ezra. There is more diversity of opinion about another omission, that of Esther. Some have thought that this was from inadvertence, either on the part of Melito or of some subsequent transcriber. This is not likely, however, as the same book is wanting in some other catalogues. Others think that it was included with Ezra and Nehemiah, which belong to the same period of the history ; but this lacks confirmation. Others find an explanation in the disputes among the Jews as to the canonicity of this book. Although those who lay most stress upon these disputations must acknowledge that at this time Esther was included in

---

[1] Four books of Kingdoms in the LXX. correspond to Samuel and Kings in the Hebrew. Westcott (p. 124) remarks : " It is evident from the names, the number, and the order of the books, that it was not taken directly from the Hebrew, but from the LXX. revised by the Hebrew." From this he infers that " the Palestinian LXX., the Greek Bible which was used by our Lord and the Apostles," contained simply the books which are found in this catalogue.

the Hebrew canon, it is possible that the suspicions thus engendered may have found a partial echo in the Christian Church; or, what is quite as probable, Melito may have been betrayed into the error of rejecting the entire book from the circumstance that the Greek Esther begins with an apocryphal section, which is not in the canon of the Jews. The list of Melito numbers 22, if reckoned according to the Jewish mode of enumeration. In common with some other catalogues, which adhere to this number, the place of Esther is supplied by counting Ruth separately instead of combining it with Judges. Apart from its omission of the Book of Esther, Melito's catalogue corresponds precisely with the books of the Old Testament as Protestants acknowledge them; and it does not contain a single one of those books which Romanists have added to the canon.

While this is the only list of the books of the Old Testament which has been preserved from the second century, other evidences are not wanting that the same canon prevailed in other parts of the Eastern Church at that time. Justin Martyr, so called because he suffered martyrdom for his faith A.D. 164, was born in Palestine, and after his conversion resided chiefly in Rome, travelled extensively, and wrote largely. He quotes freely from the canonical books, but never makes any use of the Apocrypha. And in a controversy which he had with Trypho, a Jew in Ephesus, and in which the differences between Jews and Christians are discussed at length, no allusion is made to any difference in their canon. And the old Syriac version, which, according to the opinion of the ablest critics, was made in this century, originally contained only the canonical, none of the apocryphal, books of the Old Testament.

Passing to the third century, we find another catalogue from Origen, the most learned of the Greek fathers, who was educated in Alexandria and died at Tyre, A.D. 254, at the age of 68. His catalogue, like that of Melito, is preserved by Eusebius in his "Ecclesiastical History" (VI., 25). He reckons the number of the books 22, as was done by Josephus. Having given the Hebrew and Greek names in full of those books which he esteems canonical, he adds at the close, "And apart from these" (i.e., not forming a part of the canon) "are the Books of Maccabees." In this catalogue of Origen, as we now have it, the Minor Prophets are omitted. This is evidently, however, not an omission of Origen himself, but has arisen from inaccurate transcription, for the number stated is 22, and then 21 are named, showing that one has been left out. And in the ancient Latin translation of this passage by Ruffin, the Minor Prophets are mentioned in their proper place. The catalogue of Origen, thus corrected, agrees again precisely with the canon which we possess, except in one remarkable addition, viz., that he includes in the Book of Jeremiah Lamentations and his Epistle. Some have supposed that Origen here intends the Epistle of Jeremiah addressed to the captives at Babylon, which is found in chaps. xxvii.–xxix. of the canonical book, and, of course, does belong to the canon. It is more probable, however, that he means an apocryphal epistle, bearing his name, which is found in the Vulgate as the last chapter of the Book of Baruch ; and in this case he has been betrayed into the belief that this forged letter was a genuine production of the prophet. This is a mistake, however, which is easily corrected ; for Origen, like Melito, professedly follows the Hebrew canon, and this apocryphal letter never had a place in that canon.

We have no other catalogue from this century, but we have what is equivalent to one in Tertullian, the first of the Latin fathers whose writings have been preserved. He says that the books of the Old Testament number 24, and finds a symbolical allusion to them in the 24 elders round about the throne and the 24 wings of the four living creatures spoken of in the Revelation. This is the number of the sacred books as stated in the Talmud, and in many other ancient catalogues which correspond with the Jewish canon. There can be no doubt of its identity with that canon, and it leaves no room for the admission of the Apocrypha.

We thus have in the second and third centuries testimonies from the Eastern Church in Melito and the old Syriac version, from the Greek Church in Origen, and from the Latin Church in Tertullian; and all combine to sanction the Protestant canon and to exclude the Apocrypha.

Proceeding to the fourth century, where testimonies are more abundant, we shall find the same thing corroborated from all parts of the Church. In regard to the so-called canon of Laodicea, Westcott says (p. 170): "A decree was made upon the sacred books at the Synod of Laodicea, a small gathering of clergy from parts of Lydia and Phrygia, which was held about A.D. 363. After other disciplinary ordinances the last canon runs: 'Psalms composed by private men must not be read in the Church, nor books not admitted into the canon, but only the canonical books of the New and Old Testaments.' To this decree, in the printed editions of the canons and in most MSS., a list of the holy Scriptures is added which is absolutely identical with Cyril's, except as to the position of Esther and Job, and adding Baruch and the Letter to Jeremiah. But this list is, without doubt, a later addition. It is omitted in good Greek MSS., in two distinct Syriac versions preserved in MSS. of the sixth or seventh century, in one of the two complete Latin versions, and in the oldest digests of the canons."

There are, however, catalogues of unquestioned genuineness from five individual fathers belonging to the Greek or Oriental Church, viz., from Athanasius of Alexandria, Cyril of Jerusalem, Epiphanius of Salamine in Cyprus, Amphilochius of Iconium in Asia Minor, and Gregory Nazianzen of Cappadocia, for a short time resident in Constantinople and appointed Patriarch of that city. To these may be added Basil the Great of Cappadocia and Chrysostom, the distinguished preacher and Patriarch of Constantinople; for though they have not left formal catalogues, they have made statements which may be considered equivalent, and which render sufficiently manifest what canon they adopted. For the former says [1] that the number of the books of the Old Testament was 22, as they are reckoned by Josephus and by Origen; and the latter [2] says: "All the books of the Old Testament were originally written in Hebrew, as all among us confess," which makes it plain that he followed the Jewish canon.

To these testimonies from the Greek and Oriental Church may be added three from the Latin Church, Hilary of Poitiers in France, Ruffin of Aquileia in Italy, and Jerome, the most learned man of his time, all of whom have left catalogues of the Old Testament books.

Two of these catalogues, those of Gregory Nazianzen and Athanasius, omit the Book of Esther, as was done by Melito; and the omission may be explained in the same way. Athanasius even includes Esther among the non-canonical books, adding that "it begins with Mordecai's dream," which is the beginning of the apocryphal additions. He further states that "Esther is

---

[1] Philocalia, ch. iii.   See Cosin, p. 66.
[2] Homil. iv. in Gen.   See Cosin, p. 70.

canonical among the Hebrews ; and as Ruth is reckoned
as one book with Judges, so Esther with some other
book." [1] If he is here to be understood as intimating
his own agreement with what he attributes to the
Hebrews, he may simply mean that the Greek additions
to Esther are apocryphal, and that the remainder of the
book is canonical, and considered as included in some
other constituent of the canon. Or else he has been
betrayed into the mistake of rejecting the entire book
because of these spurious additions—a mistake which
finds ample correction in other sources, which prove
beyond a doubt that Esther, freed from these spurious
chapters, rightfully belongs to the canon.

Hilary inserts in his catalogue, instead of the simple
name of Jeremiah, Jeremiah and *the Epistle*, which is to
be accounted for as the same addition in the catalogue
of Origen. And so must the addition found in two
others, those of Athanasius and Cyril : Jeremiah, *Baruch
and the Epistle*. Some have thought that parts of the
canonical Book of Jeremiah are so called, those in which
mention is made of Baruch, the personal attendant and
helper of the prophet, and in which the letter is recorded which Jeremiah wrote to the captives in Babylon. It is more probable, however, that they meant the
apocryphal Book of Baruch and the apocryphal Epistle
of Jeremiah ; and in this case they have unwittingly
given their sanction to a forgery, being misled by their
veneration for the names attached to it to give credit to
what they never wrote.

With these easily explained exceptions all the cat-
alogues above mentioned sustain the Protestant canon.
The Church of the first four centuries, Greek and Latin,
Eastern and Western, in Asia Minor, Syria, Palestine,
Alexandria, Cyprus, Constantinople, Carthage, Italy,

[1] Cosin, p. 49.

and France, testifies in favor of the same canon which prevailed among the Jews, and which received the infallible sanction of our Lord and his apostles, and which Protestants now embrace.

It is a mere evasion to say that these fathers did not design to give the Christian, but the Jewish canon. These catalogues were intended for Christian readers, to inform them in regard to the books which properly belonged to the Old Testament. They do in fact give the Jewish canon, but only because that was likewise binding on the Christian Church.

It has also been said [1] that these fathers were mistaken, but excusable, because the Church had not as yet made any formal decision in regard to the extent of the canon by a general council. But this is a question which the Church has no inherent right to determine. Her only function is to hand down faithfully what was delivered to her.

There are some testimonies near the close of the fourth century upon which great stress has been laid, as though they sanctioned the canonicity of the Apocrypha. But plausible as this may appear at first view, they do not when carefully examined lend any real support to the Romish canon, nor do they teach anything at variance with the testimony already gathered from so many witnesses. The authorities referred to are Augustin, one of the most distinguished and influential of the fathers as a theologian, but of very little ability as a critic, and the councils of Hippo and Carthage. Westcott (p. 185) says of them: "The first discussion on the canon in which Augustin took part was at a council at Hippo, in A.D. 393. The decision which was then made is lost, but the statutes of the council were revised and confirmed by the council of Carthage, in

_____
[1] Bellarmin, De Verbo Dei, I., 10.

A.D. 397. In the meantime Augustin wrote his essay 'On Christian Doctrine,' in which he treats of the books of Scripture." These catalogues of the canonical books are of a uniform tenor, containing the names not only of those in the Hebrew canon, but in addition most of those that are reckoned canonical by Romanists.[1] In regard to these catalogues it is to be observed:

1. They do not coincide precisely with the canon of Rome, either in what they admit or in what they exclude. The Book of Baruch is not found in these lists, although Romanists regard it as canonical. On the other hand,

---

[1] Augustin's catalogue is as follows (De Doctrina Christiana, II., 8): " Five of Moses, that is, Genesis, Exodus, Leviticus, Numbers, Deuteronomy, one book of Joshua, one of Judges, one little book which is called Ruth, which seems rather to belong to the beginning of Kings, then four of Kings and two of Chronicles, not following, but joined as it were alongside and going along together. This is the history which, connected throughout, contains the times and order of things. There are others, as if of a different series, which are neither connected with this series nor among themselves, as Job, and Tobit, and Esther, and Judith, and two books of Maccabees, and two of Esdras, which seem rather to follow that well-arranged history ending with Kings and Chronicles. Then the Prophets, among which are one book of David, the Psalms, and three of Solomon, Proverbs, Song of Songs, and Ecclesiastes; for those two books, one of which is entitled Wisdom and another Ecclesiasticus, are from a certain resemblance said to be Solomon's, but Jesus, the son of Sirach, is by an unbroken tradition declared to have written them [this mistake as to the authorship of Wisdom is corrected by Augustin in the second book of his Retractationes]. Since, however, they deserved to be received into authority, they are to be numbered among the prophetical books. The remainder are books which are properly called prophets—twelve individual books of prophets which, being connected together, since they are never separated, are regarded as one—the names of which prophets are these: Hosea, Joel, Amos, Micah, Nahum, Habakkuk, Obadiah, Jonah, Zephaniah, Haggai, Zechariah, Malachi. Then there are four prophets of larger volume: Isaiah, Jeremiah, Daniel, Ezekiel. With these forty-four books the authority of the Old Testament is ended."

these lists make mention of two books of Esdras. The first, according to the uniform mode of enumeration among the ancients, must embrace the books of Ezra and Nehemiah. By the second Book of Esdras in these catalogues must accordingly be intended that which in the Vulgate is numbered 3Esdras, or in the English Apocrypha 1Esdras; and this Romanists do not account canonical.

2. These are not three independent testimonies. It should be remembered that Augustin was bishop of Hippo, and Hippo lay in the vicinity of Carthage; and Augustin's influence was controlling in both these councils.

3. It is not reasonable to suppose that a different canon prevailed in Carthage and its vicinity from that which, as we have seen, was found in all the rest of the Church, and in Carthage itself at an earlier date. If, then, these catalogues can with any fairness be interpreted in a manner which shall bring them into accord with the general voice of the Church in this and preceding centuries, it certainly should be preferred to an interpretation which assumes an irreconcilable conflict between them.

4. Such an interpretation is not only possible, but it readily offers itself, and is in fact absolutely required by the language of these catalogues themselves. There is good reason to believe that by canonical books both Augustin and these councils intended, not the canon in its strict sense, as limited to those books which are inspired and divinely authoritative, but in a more lax and wider sense, as including along with these other books which, though not inspired, were sanctioned and commended by the Church as profitable and edifying religious books, and suitable both for private perusal and for public reading in the churches. That Augustin understands canonical in this lax sense is apparent.

a. As Westcott (p. 185) says: "Augustin's attention seems to have been directed toward the attainment of a conciliar determination of the contents of the Bible soon after his conversion. His former connection with the Manichees, who were especially addicted to the use of apocryphal Gospels and Acts, probably impressed him keenly with the necessity of some such decision. The wide circulation of the Manichæan books had already moved Cyril of Jerusalem to write upon the subject, and afterward led the Spanish bishops to seek the assistance of the Roman Church in checking their spread. The fact is important, for it explains the motive which may have led Augustin to hold the distinction between the 'controverted' and the 'acknowledged' books of the Old Testament as of comparatively little moment. It might have seemed well to him if both could be placed in a position wholly and forever separate from the pernicious writings which had been turned to heretical uses."

b. Augustin prefaces his catalogue in the following manner: [1] "He will be the wisest student of the divine Scriptures who shall have first read and learned . . . those which are called canonical. For he will read the rest with greater security when furnished with faith in the truth, lest they preoccupy a mind as yet unstable, and instil some ideas contrary to sound understanding by perilous fictions and fancies. In regard to the canonical Scriptures let him follow the authority of as many Catholic Churches as possible, among which assuredly are those which were deemed worthy to be apostolical sees, and to have epistles addressed to them. He will, therefore, hold this course in regard to the canonical Scriptures, that he prefer those which are received by

[1] Cosin, p. 102. I have adopted Westcott's translation of this passage.

all Catholic Churches to those which some do not receive; of those again which are not received by all, those which more and more influential Churches receive to those which are held by Churches fewer in number or inferior in authority. If, however, he find some writings maintained by more Churches, others by more influential Churches, though this case can hardly be realized, I fancy that they must be held to be of equal authority." It will be perceived that Augustin divides divine Scriptures into those which are canonical and those which contain perilous fictions and fancies. And he makes distinctions among canonical Scriptures, some being universally received, and others being ranked according to the number and influence of the Churches that do receive them. It is evident that what he calls canonical books are not all of the same grade in his esteem. He could not speak thus if he regarded them all as alike inspired of God.

c. Elsewhere in his writings Augustin uses expressions which show that he ranked the Hebrew canon above the books which in his catalogue are associated with it. Thus he says:[1] "After Malachi, Haggai, Zechariah, and Ezra, they had no prophets until the advent of the Saviour; wherefore the Lord himself says, The law and the prophets were until John." As the apocryphal books were written after prophecy had ceased, he could not regard them as inspired. He says further:[2] "Those things which are not written in the canon of the Jews cannot be adduced with so much confidence against opposers." Again he says:[3] "All those books which prophesy of Christ are with the Jews. We bring forward documents from the Jews to confound other enemies. The Jew carries the document whence the

---

[1] De Civitate Dei, XVII., last chapter.
[2] Ibid., ch. 20.   [3] On Psalm xlvi.

Christian derives his faith; they are made our libra-
rians." Again:[1] "What is written in the Book of Judith
the Jews are truly said not to have received into the
canon of Scripture." And speaking of other books of
the same class:[2] "They are not found in the canon which
the people of God received, because it is one thing to be
able to write as men with the diligence of historians,
and another as prophets with divine inspiration; the
former pertained to the increase of knowledge, the
latter to authority in religion, in which authority the
canon is kept."

d. Augustin's mind in this matter is most clearly and
unambiguously shown in what he says of the books of
Maccabees:[3] "The Jews do not have this Scripture
which is called Maccabees, as they do the law and the
prophets, to which the Lord bears testimony as to his
witnesses. But it is received by the Church not without advantage, if it be read and heard soberly, especially for the sake of the history of the Maccabees, who
suffered so much from the hand of persecutors for the
sake of the law of God." Augustin is here arguing
against the Circumcelliones, so called from their living
in cells, which they erected in various parts of the country. These were a fanatical sect, who held it to be
right to commit self-murder, and appealed in justifica-
tion to 2 Macc. xiv. 42 ff., where Razis is commended
for destroying his own life to prevent his falling into
the hands of his enemies. Augustin says, in reply:[4]
"They are in great straits for authorities, having only
this one passage to which they can appeal in all the
books sanctioned by the Church;" and this in a book

---

[1] De Civitate Dei, XVIII., ch. 26.
[2] Ibid., ch. 38.
[3] Contra Epistolam Gaudentii Donatistæ, ch. 23.
[4] Epistola 61, ad Dulcitium.

which the Jews do not receive, to which the Lord does not bear testimony, as he does to the law and the prophets, and which the Church receives, not as inspired and infallibly authoritative, but because it records the history of men who suffered nobly for the cause of God ; and it must " be read and heard soberly," *i.e.*, everything that it contains must not be accepted with implicit faith, but caution must be exercised, and Christian discretion and an enlightened conscience are necessary to distinguish what in it is right from what is wrong.   Self-murder, though approved by the Book of Maccabees, is not to be justified. Augustin also expresses himself to the same purport elsewhere : [1] " The account of the times since the restoration of the Temple is not found in the holy Scriptures which are called canonical, but in others, among which are also the books of the Maccabees, which the Jews do not, but which the Church does, esteem canonical on account of the violent and extraordinary sufferings of certain martyrs."   According to this passage, it appears that in one sense of the term the Maccabees were not canonical, in another they were ; and the Church reckoned them canonical, not because of their inspiration, but because of their recording examples of heroic martyrdom, such as would tend to nerve others to unfaltering constancy, and would be particularly useful in times of persecution. In other words, if canonical meant inspired, the Maccabees were not canonical ; if it meant books that were adapted to make a salutary religious impression, they were.   Augustin being the judge, then, these catalogues do not conflict with the general voice of the Church in this and preceding centuries regarding the canon of the Old Testament.

    5. That the Council of Carthage did not design to cut

[1] De Civitate Dei, XVIII., ch. 36.

itself off from the rest of the Church in this matter is
plain from its giving direction that the Church beyond
the sea be consulted in respect to the confirmation of its
canon.   Another council was held in Carthage A.D. 419,
and presided over by Augustin, which renewed the decree concerning the canon, and added, "Let this also
be notified to our brother and fellow priest, Boniface,
Bishop of Rome, or to other bishops of those parts, for
the purpose of confirming this canon," which is described, not as inspired books, but as books "which
by a usage derived from our fathers are to be read in
the Church."

6. That the canon of the Old Testament, as it was
received and understood in Carthage and in that region
of Africa, did not really differ from that of the rest of
the Church, and from that which Protestants now
accept, is plain from the testimony of Tertullian of
Carthage in the preceding century, who, as we have
already seen, recognized only 24 books as belonging to
the Old Testament, when its canon is understood in a
strict and proper sense as limited to the books inspired
of God.   It is apparent, likewise, from the testimony
of Primasius and Junilius, bishops in that region of
Africa in the succeeding century, circ. A.D. 550.   Primasius, commenting on the Apocalypse (ch. iv.), reckons
24 books of the Old Testament, corresponding in number to the elders and the wings of the living creatures
round about the throne.   Junilius divides divine books
into three classes: "Some are of perfect authority,
some of medium authority, and some of no authority."
His third class answers to what Augustin calls the non-
canonical divine Scriptures, with their "perilous fictions
and fancies."   The canonical books of Augustin and
the Council of Carthage are divided between the other
two classes, showing that these catalogues were not

understood to mean that they were all of the same grade.[1]

The explicit testimonies to the canon of the Old Testament in the catalogues of Christian councils and Christian fathers of the first four centuries have now been examined. And it has been found that, with the exception of three catalogues at the close of the fourth or the beginning of the fifth century, all the remainder, with slight and unimportant variations, unanimously and unambiguously sustain the Protestant canon. And the other three emanate from one region, and were issued under one influence; so that they are virtually one testimony, and this demanding an explanation which brings it, too, into harmony with the united testimony of the rest of the catalogues. There was a strict canon, limited to books inspired of God, which is witnessed to from all parts of the Church during these early ages, and is identical with the canon of Jews and with that of Protestants. But the term canon was also used in a more lax and wider sense by Augustin and the councils in his region, who embraced in it not only the inspired word, but in addition certain books which had gained a measure of sanctity in their eyes from their connection with the Greek and Latin Bible, and from their having been admitted to be read in the churches on account of their devotional character and

---

[1] The division which Junilius makes is somewhat arbitrary, and indicative of the confusion which had arisen from indiscriminately combining in these catalogues books of different character. He includes Ecclesiasticus among those of perfect authority, to which some join Wisdom and the Song of Songs. Those of medium authority are two books of Chronicles, Job, Ezra (including Nehemiah), Judith, Esther, and two books of Maccabees. That he, nevertheless, intends to give the Hebrew canon is apparent from the reason which he assigns for this partition, " Because they are received among the Hebrews with this difference, as Jerome and others testify."

the noble examples of martyrdom which they recorded. These supplementary volumes, however, were not put upon a level with the canon strictly so-called in point of authority. They were to be read and heard soberly in the exercise of Christian discretion, and with this caution they were commended to Christian people.

From the fourth century onward the leading authorities of the Greek Church, like their predecessors, in their lists of the books of the Old Testament reject the Apocrypha. Thus Anastasius, Patriarch of Antioch (A.D. 560), and Leontius of Byzantium (A.D. 580), make the number of the sacred books 22. And "John of Damascus, the last of the great Greek fathers, whose writings are still regarded with the deepest reverence in the Eastern Church . . . transcribes almost verbally one of the lists of Epiphanius, which gives only the books of the Hebrew canon as of primary authority. To these Ecclesiasticus and Wisdom are subjoined as an appendix, 'being noble and good books, though not prophetical.'" [1]

In the Western or Latin Church sentiment was divided, some following the strict canon of Jerome, others the more enlarged canon of Augustin. And Augustin's list, being taken without note of the cautions which he connected with it, led ultimately to a result which he had not intended, the effacing of the distinction between inspired and uninspired, and ranking all upon the same level. Cassiodorus, in his Institutes (A.D. 556), places the lists of Jerome and Augustin side by side without deciding between them; Isidore of Seville (A.D. 636) does the same. Among the advocates of the strict canon is one Bishop of Rome, Gregory the Great (✠ 604), who in quoting a passage from 1 Maccabees says: "We adduce a testimony from books, though not canonical, yet pub-

---

[1] Westcott, p. 222.

lished for the edification of the Church." And other distinguished men in the Western Church, forming a continuous chain of witnesses from the fourth century down to the very time of the Council of Trent, in Italy, Spain, France, England, and Germany, have given their suffrages in favor of the Hebrew canon and against the Apocrypha.[1] Even in the sixteenth century, shortly before the assembling of the Council of Trent, Cardinal Ximenes, Archbishop of Toledo in Spain, in the preface to his Complutensian Polyglott, dedicated to Pope Leo X., and approved by him, states that the books of the Old Testament there printed in Greek only, viz., Tobit, Judith, Wisdom, Ecclesiasticus, Baruch, and the Maccabees, with the additions to Esther and Daniel, were not in the canon, but were received by the Church rather for the edification of the people than for confirming the authority of ecclesiastical doctrines. And Cardinal Cajetan at Rome (✠ 1534), a theologian of great eminence, who it has been thought would have been chosen Pope if he had outlived Clement VII., was of the same mind. In the preface to his commentary on the Epistle to the Hebrews he says: "We have chosen the rule of Jerome that we may not err in distinguishing the canonical books; for those which he delivered as canonical we hold to be canonical, and those which he separated from the canonical books we hold to be out of the canon." In dedicating his Commentary on the Historical Books of the Old Testament to Clement VII. he writes: "The whole Latin Church is very greatly indebted to St. Jerome for distinguishing the canonical from the non-canonical books, since he has freed us from the reproach of the Hebrews that we frame for ourselves books or parts of books of the old

[1] These are discussed at length in Cosin's Scholastical History of the Canon.

canon which they lack entirely. For Judith, Tobit, and
the Maccabees are reckoned by Jerome to be outside of
the canonical books and placed among the Apocrypha,
along with the Book of Wisdom and Ecclesiasticus.
These are not canonical books, that is, they do not belong to the rule for confirming those things which are
of faith; yet they can be called canonical, that is, belonging to the rule for the edification of believers. With
this distinction what is said by Augustin and written by
the Council of Carthage can be rightly apprehended."

   In all this interval of more than a thousand years
there are few genuine catalogues which contain the
Apocrypha.   Two catalogues are attributed to Bishops
of Rome, Innocent I. (A.D. 405), and Gelasius (A.D. 492–
496), of which Westcott says (p. 195): "Both these lists
are open to the gravest suspicion. . . .   They were
unknown to Cassiodorus, who carefully collected the different lists of Holy Scripture current in his time, and at
a still later time to Isidore of Seville; the text of the
Gelasian list varies considerably in different copies, and
in such a way as to indicate that the variations were
not derived from one original.   The earliest historical
traces of the decretals of which they form a part are
found in the eighth century.   The letter of Innocent
was sent to Charlemagne in A.D. 774 by Hadrian I., in
the Code of Ecclesiastical Law, and from that time it
exercised some influence upon the judgment of the
Church.   The list of the canonical books in the decree
of Gelasius does not distinctly appear till about the
tenth century, and even in later times was comparatively little known. . . .   Both lists simply repeat
the decision at Carthage and determine the ecclesiastical canon, the books, that is, which might be publicly
used in the Church services."[1]

[1] See also Cosin, pp. 118–128.

The council at Florence (A.D. 1439), which was chiefly
occupied with settling the disputes between the Eastern
and Western Churches, is also said to have issued a
catalogue corresponding with that at Carthage.   But
the reality of this is likewise disputed.[1]

The Council of Trent, which Roman Catholics regard
as an œcumenical council, and consequently authoritative in all its decrees, in its fourth session, April 8, 1546,
adopted the following: "The Synod doth receive and
venerate all the books as well of the Old as of the New
Testament, since one God is the author of both, also
the unwritten traditions pertaining to faith and morals,
as proceeding from the mouth of Christ or dictated by
the Holy Spirit, with an equal feeling of piety and reverence."   The list of the sacred books is then given,
including Tobit, Judith, Wisdom, Ecclesiasticus, Baruch, and two books of Maccabees.   The decree concludes : "If any one does not receive these books entire,
with all their parts,[2] as they are accustomed to be read
in the Catholic Church, and knowingly and intelligently
despises the traditions aforesaid, let him be anathema."
The novel features of this decree are : That the apocryphal books and unwritten traditions are here affirmed
to be upon a par with the strictly canonical books, and
that an anathema is pronounced upon those who hold a
contrary view.   There was a great diversity of opinion
in the council as to the best method of dealing with the
subject of the canon.   Some proposed simply to make a
list of books sanctioned by the Church, as was done at
Carthage, without pronouncing upon their relative
value; others desired to follow the example of Jerome
and make two lists, one belonging strictly to the canon

[1] Westcott, p. 199; Cosin, pp. 180–188.
[2] This is intended to cover the apocryphal portions of Esther and
Daniel.

and the other of books commended as edifying, but not to be used in proof of doctrines; a third class insisted upon the course which finally prevailed. The decision turned at last not upon a thorough examination of the question upon its merits, but upon the existing usage of the Church of Rome, which had selected its lessons from the Apocrypha as well as from the canonical Scriptures, and upon a desire to make an issue with the Protestants, who had planted themselves upon the Hebrew canon as sanctioned by the Lord and his apostles.

The formal and explicit testimony of the Church on the subject of the canon, as given in its catalogues and express statements, has now been reviewed from the beginning to the time of the Council of Trent, with its evidence unequivocally in favor of the strict Protestant view. But alongside of this deliberate testimony formally given to the sharp distinction between the apocryphal and canonical books, there grew up in popular usage a sort of indiscriminate treatment of them as alike promotive of piety and conducive to spiritual edification. The Apocrypha were more or less permeated with the spirit of the Old Testament, dealt with the fortunes of the chosen people and God's gracious care exercised over them, inculcated devotion toward God and steadfast adherence to his service, as well as integrity and uprightness in the affairs of life, and were at a vast remove from the pagan and polytheistic literature which abounded everywhere. It is not strange, therefore, that they came to be classed with sacred religious literature as opposed to pagan and heretical productions, and that in ordinary usage the distinction between them and the strictly canonical books seems to be sometimes obscured; though when the question of their relative value is raised, this distinction is always clearly marked. Advantage has been taken of this popular usage, and the attempt made to show that it reflects a belief on the part of the early Church in the canonicity and inspiration of the Apocrypha, which, it is urged, must nullify or materially modify the direct and positive assertions already produced of a contrary belief. Three particulars are here alleged as justifying this conclusion, viz. :

1. The Apocrypha were included in the early versions of the Scriptures.

2. They were read in the churches in public worship.

3. They were quoted by the fathers as divinely authoritative.

In regard to the first allegation, that the Apocrypha were included in the early versions of the Scriptures, and must, therefore, have been regarded as a part of the word of God, it is obvious to remark :

(1.) The Apocrypha were not included in all the early versions. It was not in the Syriac Peshitto. It was not Jerome's original intention to translate any of these books in his Latin version, though he was subsequently persuaded to change his mind in respect to Tobit and Judith, while not esteeming them canonical. The rest of the Apocrypha as found in the Latin Vulgate is taken from an earlier version known as the Itala.

(2.) It has already been shown that, though these books came to be included in the Septuagint at some date now unknown, they were there only as an appendage to the inspired books, and not as equal to them in inspiration and authority; for the Alexandrian Jews, amongst whom that version circulated and for whom it was prepared, never admitted them to the canon. Now since the earlier translations were for the most part made from the Greek rather than the Hebrew, it is natural that all that was in the Greek version should be translated. If they were allowed to be connected with the Septuagint without being thought to be inspired, why might they not be retained in translations made from that version without an assertion of their canonicity? They were not reckoned a part of the infallible word, but they were revered and valued, and possessed a sort of sacredness from their resemblance to and their association with the Holy Scriptures.

(3.) The Romish argument inverts the real order of the facts, and makes that the cause which was rather the effect. It is not the canonicity of these books which led to their insertion in the Septuagint and other versions, but their incorporation with these versions which led in certain quarters to their admission to the canon, when this was understood in a lax and improper sense. And it may easily have led in some cases to their being regarded with a consideration to which they were not entitled. The fathers reading Greek and Latin, but being unacquainted with Hebrew, might, on finding these books in the Greek and Latin Bible, and not being aware of their exclusion from the Hebrew canon, ignorantly attribute to them an authority which they do not possess.

(4.) The analogy of modern versions of the Scriptures also shows that the Apocrypha may be included in them without being regarded as a part of the inspired Word of God. In Luther's translation of the Bible the Apocrypha are added as an appendix to the Old Testament, with the heading, "These are books which are not esteemed like the Holy Scriptures, and yet are useful and good to read." The Apocrypha were similarly inserted in King James's translation of the English Bible, though the translators did not consider them a part of the canon.

(5.) If this argument is urged, it will prove more than Romanists themselves are willing to admit. Books which they reject as uncanonical and uninspired, and which in fact no one has ever dreamed of including in the canon, are contained in ancient versions. The Septuagint contains 3d Esdras (E. V. 1st Esdras) and 3d Maccabees. In the Vulgate itself, which the Council of Trent pronounced authentic, are 3d and 4th Esdras and the Prayer of Manasseh. And the old Ethiopic version contains the Book of Enoch, the Ascension of Isaiah, the Book of Jubilees, and others which are similarly destitute of authority.[1] Why are not these in the canon, if existence in an ancient version is sufficient to prove that it is entitled to a place there?

As to the allegation that the Apocrypha were read in the churches along with the canonical books of Scripture, it is to be observed:

(1.) While the fact is to a certain extent admitted, the argument based upon it is unsound. All depends upon the meaning and intention with which this was done. This is not to be judged by modern ideas and practice, but by the ideas and practice of the early Church in this respect.

(2.) That a clear distinction was made between canonical books and books which were read in the churches appears from the most explicit testimony. Thus Jerome says:[2] "As therefore the Church reads the books of Judith, Tobit, and Maccabees, but does not receive them among the canonical Scriptures, so it also reads these two volumes [Wisdom and Ecclesiasticus] for the edification of the people, but not for authority to prove the

---

[1] Westcott, p. 238, mentions an Ethiopic catalogue of the Old Testament in the British Museum which, in addition to the canonical books and the Greek Apocrypha, has "the apocryphal story of Asenath, the wife of Joseph, the Book of Jubilees, a strange Judaic commentary on Genesis, and an unknown apocryphal writing, Ozias."

[2] Cosin, p. 46. Thornwell, Arguments of Romanists Discussed and Refuted, p. 299.

doctrines of religion." Ruffin, a contemporary of Jerome, says :[1] "It should, however, be known that there
are other books which were called by our forefathers
not canonical, but ecclesiastical, as the Wisdom of Solomon and another so-called Wisdom of the Son of
Sirach. . . . Of the same rank is the Book of Tobit,
and Judith, and the Books of the Maccabees. . . .
All which they would have read in the Church, but not
adduced for confirming the authority of the faith.   Other
writings they named apocryphal,[2] which they would not
have read in the Church.   These things, as I have said,
have been delivered to us from the fathers."   To the
same purport is the language of Athanasius :[3] "All the
Scripture of us Christians is divinely inspired.   It contains books that are not indefinite, but comprised in a
fixed canon."   Then, after enumerating the books in detail, he proceeds : "But besides these books there are
also some others of the Old Testament not indeed received into the canon, but which are only read before
the catechumens.   These are Wisdom, Sirach or Ecclesiasticus, Esther, Judith, and Tobit.   These are not
canonical."   Augustin is quoted by Cosin, p. 106, as
saying that the Book of Wisdom was deemed fit to read
from the reader's desk, but not from that of the bishops
or the pulpit.   These explicit testimonies, and others of
like tenor which might be adduced if necessary, make it
certain that there were books approved as suitable to
be read in the churches which yet were not regarded
as canonical.

[1] In Symbol. Apostol., 36.   Cosin, p. 88.   Thornwell, ubi supra.

[2] Ruffin uses " apocryphal " in the sense of heretical and pernicious,
as opposed not merely to canonical, but also to ecclesiastical, which
latter corresponds to " apocryphal " as commonly used in the discussion of the canon.

[3] Synopsis Sac. Script.   Cosin, pp. 48, 49.   Thornwell, p. 321.

(3.) The present practice of the Church of England in this matter sufficiently shows that to direct to be read in the churches and to esteem canonical are not necessarily convertible expressions. The Apocrypha are enjoined to be read in public worship " for example of life and instruction of manners," but at the same time expressly declared not to be a part of the canon. Lessons are accordingly selected from these as well as from the canonical books ; only they are read upon other days than the Sabbath.

(4.) This argument, also, if valid, will prove too much, for books such as Esdras and Hermas were admitted to be read in ancient churches which Rome does not account canonical.

It is alleged still further that the apocryphal books are quoted and referred to by the early fathers in a manner which shows that they were esteemed canonical. This is the most plausible ground that can be urged, for these books are cited loosely in a way which, if we had not convincing evidence to the contrary, might lead us to suppose that they were esteemed to be a part of the inspired Word of God. It must first be ascertained whether what is alleged as a quotation from the Apocrypha is really such, for many pretended citations turn out upon examination to be no citations at all, but have only that remote resemblance which might attach to the expressions of different writers independently conceived. And, if it be a real quotation, it must be ascertained whether it is cited in such a manner as to show that the writer esteemed it to be the inspired Word of God ; otherwise he may have quoted it as he would quote any human production.

In regard to the writings of the Christians of the first century, or, as they are commonly called, the Apostolical Fathers, Westcott sums up the case thus : " Clement

uses the narrative of Judith in exactly the same manner as that of Esther; and Barnabas, as might have
been expected from an Alexandrian writer, appears to
have been familiar with Wisdom and Ecclesiasticus,
and he quotes the second Book of Esdras (4th Esdras)
as the work of a prophet. The reference of Clement to
Wisdom and of Polycarp to Tobit are very doubtful."
These fathers may have been acquainted with some
books of the Apocrypha, and have believed that Judith
was a true history; but it does not follow that they put
them on a par with the inspired writings. If Barnabas
thought that 2d Esdras, a book which is not in the
Roman Catholic canon, was written by Ezra, he was
mistaken.

By the fathers from the second century onward the
Apocrypha are freely quoted, but so are the books of
uninspired and heathen writers, as Homer, Virgil,
Cicero, etc. A bare citation shows nothing more than
that the book was known and contained something per-
tinent to the subject in hand. It gives no information
respecting the authority accorded to it and the esteem
in which it was held.

Another large class of citations is quite as little to
our present purpose, viz., those in which these books
are spoken of with respect, the sentiments which they
contain are quoted with approbation or their histories
appealed to as true. There is a very wide difference
between holding that a book contains much that is excellent and worthy of regard, or that it records historical
facts, and accepting it as the inspired Word of God.
Unless there is something in the mode of citation
which implies the inspiration or divine authority of the
volume quoted, it proves nothing to the purpose. It
is urged, however, that this is repeatedly done by the
fathers.

1. They make use of the same formulas in quoting from the Apocrypha that they do in quoting from the canonical books, and they frequently apply to the former names and epithets which are appropriate to the latter.

2. They speak of the writers of these books in the same terms which they employ in relation to the inspired writers.

Citations from the Apocrypha are introduced by the words, " It is written," which is the common formula in the New Testament in quoting from the Old, and which became the established phrase in citing from the inspired writings. And such titles as Scripture, sacred Scripture, holy Scripture, divine Scripture, are repeatedly applied to the Apocrypha as to the canonical writings. But in regard to this it should be remembered—

(1.) Although the word Scripture from long and familiar usage suggests at once to our minds the inspired volume, it is in its original import a general term, γραφή, scriptura, denoting *writing*, and applicable to any composition whatever. And in this sense it was very generally employed; thus Eusebius speaks of the Scripture of Josephus and the Scripture of Aristeas. So, too, the expression sacred or divine Scripture, need mean no more than a writing upon sacred or divine subjects —in other words, a religious book. And the fathers, in giving such titles to these books, may have meant no more than to designate them as belonging to the category of sacred in contrast with profane literature, or books upon secular subjects. And there was the more reason for using these titles in application to books which were associated with the sacred volume in the versions in most common use, and which had a sort of ecclesiastical sanction in their being allowed to be read in conjunction with the inspired books in public worship. It was to be expected that they would, in consequence, be regarded with a respect and veneration which was not felt for other human productions. And if even the term "canonical" could be applied to them in a loose and improper sense, as we have already seen, it is not surprising if a like extension was given to other terms descriptive of the sacred books.

(2.) That these terms are applied to the Apocrypha in the general sense suggested by their etymology, or else in the loose and improper sense just spoken of, is convincingly shown by the fact that the same writers who in their works distinctly exclude these books from the canon, yet cite them under these very titles. Tertullian acknowledges but 24 books of Scripture—in other words, the Hebrew canon—and yet he quotes from Baruch, Wisdom, and Ecclesiasticus. Origen, in his catalogue of the canon, leaves out the Apocrypha, yet he quotes the Wisdom of Solomon, Ecclesiasticus, Tobit, Judith, and Maccabees under the name of Scripture or the divine word. The canon of Jerome, in all three of his catalogues, is identical with that of the Hebrew Bible; yet he quotes Maccabees as Scripture, and in one place Ecclesiasticus as Holy Scripture. Chrysostom received only the Hebrew canon, yet he quotes Baruch, Ecclesiasticus, and Wisdom as divine Scripture. Athanasius adheres to the Hebrew canon in his catalogue, and yet cites the Book of Wisdom as Scripture, and Ecclesiasticus in one place as Holy Scripture and in another with the formula, "As the Holy Ghost saith." These loose, popular citations, made perhaps in some instances without distinctly remembering in what books they were to be found, should not be held to prove a belief in the inspiration of books which in their formal statements they expressly disavow and repudiate. It is much more rea-

sonable to receive their formal statements on this subject as explanatory of the sense in which they designed
their less explicit expressions to be understood.

(3.) The wide sense in which such terms as divine
books were popularly used is apparent from expressions
already quoted from Augustin, who includes among
divine books those which contain "perilous fictions
and fancies;" and from Junilius, who speaks of some
divine books as having no authority at all. Cyprian
quotes a passage from the Apocrypha as Scripture, and
then proceeds to prove the correctness of its statement
by what he calls "the testimony of truth," adducing
for that purpose the Acts of the Apostles. It is plain
that these are not put by him upon the same level.

(4.) An analogy in modern times may be found in
the fact that the Homilies of the Church of England
cite the Book of Wisdom as Scripture and as the Word
of God; and yet this book forms no part of the canon
of that Church.

(5.) Books are cited under these names which none
esteem and none ever have esteemed canonical. These
same epithets are found applied to the so-called Apostolical Constitutions, the writings of Ignatius and of
Augustin, the decrees of the Council of Nice, the Sybil-
line verses, etc.

The remaining class of citations which is urged as
decisive of the point at issue comprises those in which
the writers of these books are called by some title appropriate to inspired men, such as "prophet," or in
which the authorship of these books is ascribed to
some writer of known inspiration. Thus the Wisdom
of Solomon is frequently quoted with the formula,
"Solomon says," or "The prophet says." And mention
is made of "five books of Solomon." But—

(1.) These expressions are employed in a loose and

popular sense. This is distinctly declared by Augustin, who says: "Solomon prophesied in his books, three of which are received into canonical authority—Proverbs, Ecclesiastes, and the Song of Songs. But two others, one of which is called Wisdom and the other Ecclesiasticus, have come to be commonly called Solomon's on account of some similarity of style. Yet the more learned do not doubt that they are not his." So when the apocryphal additions to the Book of Daniel are cited under the name of Daniel, this is merely giving to a book the name popularly attributed to it. And when the Book of Baruch is cited under the name of Jeremiah, this is because Baruch was regarded as a sort of appendix to the canonical book.

(2.) If, however, the letter of these expressions is pressed, the only consequence will be not to establish the canonicity of these books, but to prove that the fathers were mistaken; for it is capable of satisfactory demonstration that Solomon was not the author of Wisdom, nor Daniel of the apocryphal chapters that are found only in the Greek, and Ecclesiasticus expressly claims to have been written by another than Solomon, and Baruch by another than Jeremiah.

(3.) That the more intelligent of the fathers did not seriously mean by these loose citations to sanction these books as the work of inspired men appears from their elsewhere declaring in a more formal way precisely the reverse. Those who were not well informed may, under the circumstances, easily have been betrayed into error in this matter.

(4.) Baruch is called a prophet in the Homilies of the Church of England, although that Church does not accept Baruch as canonical.

(5.) Books are quoted similarly which are not in the

canon of the Council of Trent, *e.g.*, 3d and 4th Esdras, under the name of the Prophet Esdras or Ezra.

The history of the canon in the Christian Church since the Council of Trent can be briefly stated. As Roman Catholics acknowledge the authority of that council, the canonicity of the Apocrypha has ever since been an established dogma in that communion. It was not to be expected, therefore, that the line of witnesses against their inspiration, which reached down to the very assembling of this council, would be continued further in that Church. Yet a few learned Romanists, such as Dupin, Jahn, and Bernard Lamy, sought to reconcile the terms of its decree with the sentiments of the primitive Church, and, while in form assenting to the former, still to maintain their accordance with the latter by making a distinction between the proto-canonical and the deutero-canonical, books. The Hebrew canon was called proto-canonical, or the first canon, and was regarded as in the fullest sense inspired and authoritative. The second canon consisted of the books added by the Council of Trent, which were held to be inferior in authority to the first, possessing a sacredness and entitled to veneration from the esteem with which they were anciently regarded and the measure of ecclesiastical sanction which they enjoyed, being read for edification in public worship, but not alleged in proof of doctrines. This, however, does not accord with the language of the decree, which puts these books on a par with the rest of the Old Testament. Accordingly, the doctrine now universally accepted in the Church of Rome assigns equal authority to the Apocrypha with the other books of the canon.

In the Greek Church the Confession of Faith by Cyril Lucar, Patriarch of Constantinople, issued in 1631, sanctions the Hebrew canon. With this agree the Confession of his friend Metrophanes Critopulus, the Orthodox Teaching of Platon, Metropolitan of Moscow, A.D. 1836, and the authorized Russian Catechism. On the other hand, the Confession of Dositheus, Patriarch of Jerusalem, prepared under Romish influence in 1672, and in opposition to the views of Lucar, sanctioned the Apocrypha.

The Protestant churches have from the first been unanimous in adhering to the Hebrew canon, which is the canon of Christ and the writers of the New Testament, and the canon of the early Church. There has, however, been some diversity among them in regard to the esteem in which they were disposed to hold the Apocrypha. This may be represented by the articles of the Church of England on the one hand, and the Westminster Confession on the other. The former repeat with approval the language of Jerome: "The Church doth read" the Apocrypha "for example of life and instruction of manners; but yet doth it not apply them to establish any doctrine." The Westminster Confession, ch. i., § 3, says: "The books commonly called Apocrypha, not being of divine inspiration, are no part of the canon of Scripture; and therefore are of no authority in the Church of God, nor to be otherwise approved or made use of than other human writings." The former of these views naturally led to their retention in the volume of the Old Testament, if not mingled indiscriminately with the canonical books, as in the Vulgate and Romish Bibles generally, yet separated from them and brought together in a sort of appendix at the end. The view of the Westminster Confession would logically banish them from the volume of Holy Scripture altogether, and treat them precisely as all other uninspired productions.

The antagonism of these two sets of opinions culmi-

nated in the famous apocryphal controversy which for
several years agitated the British and Foreign Bible
Society. In circulating the Bible in Germany, the
Society at first purchased and made use of the Canstein
Bible, which contained Luther's version of the Apocrypha as well as the canonical books. This fact being
brought to the attention of the Society in 1811, it was
resolved that its auxiliaries upon the Continent should
be requested to leave out the Apocrypha. The opposition which this met with led to the rescinding of this
order in 1813. The strife thus begun became more ar-
dent in 1819, when the Society undertook the printing
of Catholic Bibles in Italian, Spanish, and Portuguese.
The apocryphal books were in these not merely printed
as such at the end of the Old Testament, but were mingled indiscriminately with the other books, as though
they were equally part of the canon. Still, it was contended that the Society would forego all opportunity of
distributing the Scriptures in the Catholic countries of
Europe if it did not retain the Apocrypha. In 1822
the compromise was proposed and carried that the
money of the Society should only be used for printing
the canonical Scriptures, and that such auxiliaries as
chose to publish the Apocrypha should do so at their
own expense. In September, 1824, Leander Van Ess,
publisher of the Vulgate, asked the aid of the Society
in issuing an edition of the Latin Bible, promising that
he would bear the whole cost of the Apocrypha. The
sum of £500 was voted for this purpose. But in the
following December the resolution was reconsidered
and the grant withdrawn, and the Society resolved that
in future it would only aid in printing those Bibles in
which the Apocrypha was kept distinct from the canonical books. Still, these half-way measures could not
satisfy those whose consciences were offended by the

intrusion of human and uninspired productions in the volume of God's Word. The agitation was accordingly continued, until finally, on May 3, 1827, it was resolved "that no association or individual circulating the apocryphal books should receive aid from the Society; that none but bound books should be distributed to the auxiliaries, and that the auxiliaries should circulate them as received; and that all societies printing the apocryphal books should place the amount granted them for Bibles at the disposal of the parent Society."[1]

[1] Abridged from the article entitled " Bible Societies," in Appleton's Cyclopædia, which was chiefly based upon the account given in Hertzog.

XI

THE APOCRYPHA CONDEMNED BY INTERNAL EVIDENCE

THE limits of the canon must be determined mainly by external evidence; for it is a historical question: What books were committed to the Church and received by her as her rule of faith and life? To undertake to settle the canon by internal evidence exclusively would end in making it insecure, and subjecting it to capricious and arbitrary treatment. Historical questions can only be determined by historical evidence.

But while this is so, a negative value attaches to internal evidence, which may be of such a nature as to be quite decisive. A book which contains what is false in fact or erroneous in doctrine, or which is unworthy of God, cannot have been inspired by him. If these books be tried by this evident test, they will be found wanting.[1]

The books of Tobit and Judith abound in geographical, chronological, and historical mistakes, so as not only to vitiate the truth of the narratives which they contain, but to make it doubtful whether they even rest upon a basis of fact. They tend to promote superstition; they justify deception and falsehood; they make salvation and the pardon of sin to depend upon meritorious deeds, which may be purely formal and external.

It is said to have been in the youth of Tobit that the ten tribes revolted from Judah under Jeroboam, Tobit i. 4, 5; this would make him two hundred and seventy years old at the time of the Assyrian captivity. But

[1] Keerl die Apokryphen, from which the following is largely drawn.

according to xiv. 11 he was only one hundred and fifty-eight years old when he died, and according to the Latin text only one hundred and two. Contrary to all analogy of angels' visits, which are always brief as recorded in Scripture, an angel is made to journey on foot with Tobias three hundred miles. He also tells a falsehood about himself, professing (v. 12) to be one Azarias, a son of one of Tobit's acquaintances, and (vii. 3) one of the captives of the tribe of Naphtali. He afterward makes himself known as the angel Raphael (xii. 15), and teaches a doctrine which has no support elsewhere in Scripture, and which conflicts with the mediatorial office of the Lord Jesus Christ, that there are seven holy angels which present the prayers of the saints and which go in and out before the glory of the Holy One (comp. ver. 12). This notion is in all likelihood borrowed from the seven Amshaspands of the Persian superstition. An evil spirit is fantastically represented as in love with a woman, and so jealous as to murder whoever marries her (vi. 14); but the smoking heart and liver of a fish have such magical virtue as to drive this demon away (vi. 7, 17). Ch. xii. 9 ascribes to almsgiving such virtue as to deliver from death and to purge away all sin; so also iv. 10, xiv. 10, 11.

Bethulia, the scene of the Book of Judith vi. 10, 11, is a place of whose existence there is no other evidence; its significant name, meaning *virgin*, suggests that the whole story may be an allegory or romance. And no time can be found in Jewish history for the events which it records, or the protracted peace which is said to have followed. The march imputed to Holofernes is a most extraordinary zigzag. Nebuchadnezzar is said to have reigned in Nineveh (i. 1), whereas Babylon was his capital; and Joiakim is said to have been the contemporary high priest (iv. 6, xv. 8), whereas there

was no high priest of this name until after the exile, and
then Nebuchadnezzar and Nineveh and the kingdom of
the Medes (i. 1) had all passed away. Judith's language
and conduct is a continued course of falsehood and
deception, and yet it is represented as approved of God,
and she is divinely assisted in it. She even prays to
God to aid her in her deception (ix. 10, 13). The crime
of Simeon, which is condemned in Gen. xlix. 5 ff., is ap-
plauded (ix. 2). And with all these offences against the
moral law, a breach of the ceremonial, even for the sake
of preserving human life, is represented as a deadly sin
(xi. 10 ff.).

The Wisdom of Solomon and the Book of Ecclesiasticus contain many excellent maxims, and yet the moral-
ity which they inculcate is defective and is based mainly
on expediency, without a due regard to the holiness of
God or the requirements of his law. The wisdom which
they contain is not that of Solomon, but of the Alexandrian philosophy. The doctrine of emanation seems to
be taught (Wisd. vii. 25); and the pre-existence of souls,
whose mortal destiny is determined by their character
prior to their birth into this world (viii. 19, 20); and the
creation of the world, not from nothing, but out of pre-
existent matter (xi. 17). The material body is spoken of
as a weight and clog upon the soul (ix. 15), a doctrine
which has no countenance in Scripture. Israel is represented as a righteous person, and all God's favors in
their past history as a reward of their goodness (x. 15–
20), whereas in the Scriptures these are always spoken of
as undeserved mercies, bestowed in spite of their unfaith-
fulness. The miracles are exaggerated in a way that
has no sanction in the inspired narrative of them, from
a mere love of the marvellous. Thus the manna is said
(xvi. 20, 21) to have agreed to every taste, and to have
tempered itself to every man's liking; and the plagues

of Egypt are related (ch. xvi., xvii.) with a number of embellishments existing only in the imagination of the writer. A false explanation is given of the symbolical meaning of the high priest's dress (xviii. 24, 25), and a virtue attributed to it which was due only to his office and his official mediation. Cain's murder of Abel is said to have been the cause of the flood (x. 4), and a very superficial account is given of the origin of idolatry, which is traced (xiv. 15) to fathers making images of their deceased children, entirely overlooking the great moral causes which the apostle points out in Rom. i. 21–23—the alienation of the heart from God so darkening the understanding that men changed the glory of the uncorruptible God into an image made like to corruptible man and to birds and four-footed beasts and creeping things. The Book of Wisdom, moreover, claims to have been written by Solomon (ch. vii., ix. 7, 8), and yet the people of God are spoken of as in subjection to their enemies (xv. 14), which never occurred in Solomon's days; and the book was, as is evident, originally written not in Hebrew, but in Greek.

Ecclesiasticus, with much that is commendable, contains also quite a number of passages that are at variance with the spirit and teachings of the inspired word. Thus it says that almsgiving makes atonement for sin (iii. 30). Generosity to the wicked is prohibited (xii. 4–7), cruelty to slaves is justified (xxxiii. 26, 28, xlii. 5), and hatred to the Samaritans (l. 25, 26). Expediency is substituted for right as the ground of obligation, and exhortations given to do what will gain the favor of men in place of a single regard to what is acceptable in the sight of God. Thus, xxxviii. 17, "Weep bitterly for the dead for a day or two, lest thou be evil spoken of."

Baruch purports to have been written by Baruch,

the helper of Jeremiah, though it was probably written in the Greek language in whole or in part. It contains passages imitated or quoted from Daniel and Nehemiah, who lived later. According to i. 14 this book was required to be read in the house of the Lord on feasts and solemn days ; but there is no trace of such a custom having ever been observed by the Jews   Baruch is said to have been in Babylon, though he went with Jeremiah into Egypt after the capture of Jerusalem by Nebuchadnezzar.   The Temple is spoken of as standing, and offerings said to be made in Jerusalem (i. 7–10), though the Temple was burned when the city was taken. The vessels of the Temple are said to have been sent back from Babylon in the time of Jeremiah (i. 8), though they were not in fact returned until after the exile was over (Ezra i. 7).   God is spoken of as hearing the prayers of the dead (iii. 4), which, like 2 Macc. xv. 14, where Jeremiah prays for the people after his death, has been used as a proof-text for soliciting the prayers of departed saints.   The epistle of Jeremiah, which now appears as the last chapter of the Book of Baruch, is probably older than this book and by a different author. It conflicts with the genuine writings of Jeremiah in declaring that the captivity was to last seven generations, instead of seventy years, ver. 3.

1 Maccabees contains historical and geographical errors, which it is not worth while to detail here, but is much more reliable than 2 Maccabees, which abounds in legends and fables, as that of the miraculous preservation of the sacred fire (i. 19 ff.), Jeremiah's hiding the Tabernacle with the ark and altar of incense in Mount Nebo (ii. 4 ff.), the apparition which prevented Heliodorus from invading the sanctity of the Temple (iii. 25), etc.   It justifies suicide (xiv. 41–46), and prayers and offerings for the dead (xii. 41–45).   And the writer

does not claim inspiration, but only to have written according to his ability (xv. 38, 39).

The genuine Book of Esther is written in Hebrew and found in the Hebrew canon, but the additions are only in the Greek and in the old Latin version. Some writer appears, as is remarked by Jerome, to have undertaken to add what might have been said by the various persons mentioned in the book under the circumstances there described. But in so doing he interrupts the connection, contradicts the genuine chapters in various particulars, and adds others which are exceedingly improbable or evidently untrue.

The additions to the Book of Daniel consist of three parts : 1. The prayer of the three children, Shadrach, Meshach and Abednego, in the fiery furnace, which is a devout meditation, but without any special adaptation to the occasion or their situation ; and it contains (vs. 23–27) some particulars not warranted by the genuine narrative. 2. The story of Susannah, which contains a play upon words, showing that it must have been written in Greek. 3. The legend of Bel and the Dragon, which is an absurd and ridiculous fiction.

XII

ORDER AND NUMBER OF THE CANONICAL BOOKS

BLOCH, p. 137, infers from the concluding verses of Ecclesiastes that this book stood last in the original arrangement of the canon. Following a conjecture of Krochmal and Graetz, he regards Eccl. xii. 12–14 as no part of the book itself, but a note appended to the completed canon by its collectors, certifying that it sufficiently sets forth all that man requires to know in regard to his duty and his destiny, and warning against the endless multitude of other books as only wearisome, without being able to give a satisfactory response to these great questions. As there is no good reason for attributing these verses to the collectors of the canon, or understanding them as anything else than a fitting conclusion to the book itself, the inference as to its position in the canon falls of course.

An opinion much more widely entertained is that certain passages in the New Testament show that in the time of our Lord the books were arranged as they are in Hebrew Bibles at present. Thus, Mat. xxiii. 35, Luke xi. 51, in speaking of "all the righteous blood shed upon the earth," our Lord particularizes "from the blood of righteous Abel unto the blood of Zachariah, son of Barachiah, whom ye slew between the sanctuary and the altar" (cf. 2 Chron. xxiv. 20, 21). From this it has been inferred that Chronicles must have been then, as now, the last book in the Hebrew canon, since one example is taken from Genesis and the

other from Chronicles, to represent all that are recorded in the Bible from first to last. And this, though
the murder of a prophet later in point of time might
have been found in that of Uriah, the contemporary of
Jeremiah (Jer. xxvi. 23). Plausible as this argument
seems, it can scarcely be called convincing, for two
reasons : 1. From Genesis to Chronicles, considered as
the earliest and the latest of the historical books, would
be equally comprehensive, irrespective of the position
of the latter in the arrangement of the canon. And 2.
It is perhaps not absolutely certain that Zachariah, the
son of Barachiah, of Matthew, is the same as Zachariah,
the son of Jehoiada, in Chronicles.

Our Lord's words (Luke xxiv. 44) "All things must
needs be fulfilled which were written in the law of Moses, and the prophets, and the psalms concerning me,"
have been thought to indicate that the Psalms then,
as now, was the first book in the third division of the
canon, and as such is here used to denote all that is
included in that division. But the Psalms in this passage mean simply the particular book so called, which is
singled out from the rest of the Hagiographa as making
the fullest disclosures respecting Christ; so that nothing
can be inferred from it respecting the arrangement of
the books in that division of the canon.

The books of Moses and the Former Prophets, or the
historical books from Joshua to Kings, preserve one un-
varying order in all the early lists of the canon, which is
determined by their chronological succession. The Lat-
ter Prophets, or the strictly prophetical books and the
Hagiographa, are variously arranged. The order of the
Latter Prophets in the Talmudic tract Baba Bathra is
Jeremiah, Ezekiel, Isaiah, the Twelve; and that of the
Hagiographa, Ruth, Psalms, Job, Proverbs, Ecclesiastes,
Song of Songs, Lamentations, Esther, Ezra, Chronicles.

Various reasons have been assigned for the position here accorded to Isaiah:

1. The explanation offered in the Talmud is that the Books of Kings end in desolation, Jeremiah is all desolation, Ezekiel begins in desolation and ends in consolation, Isaiah is all consolation. Hence like is joined with like, desolation with desolation, and consolation with consolation.

2. Modern critics from the time of Eichhorn[1] have sought to find in it a confirmation of their views respecting the composite character of the Book of Isaiah, as partly the genuine production of the prophet, and partly belonging to the later years of the Babylonish exile. But that the authors of this passage had no such meaning is apparent from their statement that "Hezekiah and his associates wrote the Book of Isaiah," see p. 94, showing that they attributed it to the lifetime of Hezekiah and consequently of the prophet himself. And nearly four centuries previously the author of the Book of Ecclesiasticus (xlviii. 24, 25; cf. Isa. xl. 1, xlii. 9) makes it evident that Isa. xl.–lxvi was at that time regarded as the work of the prophet Isaiah; and he names the prophets in the following order: Isaiah, Jeremiah, Ezekiel, and the Twelve (xlix. 6–10).

3. Herzfeld (III. p. 103) thinks that the books of the Prophets are arranged according to their respective length: Jeremiah as the longest stands first, Ezekiel next, Isaiah next, and the Minor Prophets, constituting one book, which is shorter still, stand last. The treatises

---

[1] Einleitung, 4th Edition, p. 50; Dillmann, p. 452, note; Strack, p. 433; Davidson, Canon of the Bible, pp. 93, 94; Fürst, p. 16, who, while professedly tracing early Jewish tradition, everywhere mingles with it his own critical notions, proposes to alter the text of the passage under consideration into accordance with them, claiming that its original form may have been "Isaiah (I.), Jeremiah, Ezekiel, Isaiah (II.)."

in the several divisions of the Mishnah are arranged on
this principle.[1]

4. König (Einleitung, p. 459, note) seeks a reason
for this arrangement of the Prophets in the respective
distances to which they were enabled to penetrate the
future.

5. Marx (p. 36) proposes the explanation that the
Book of Jeremiah was placed before the other prophets
that it might stand next to Kings, of which, according
to Baba Bathra, he was the author; Ezekiel follows as
his junior contemporary; Isaiah is thus brought into
conjunction with Hosea, the first of the Minor Prophets,
who (Isa. i. 1; Hos. i. 1) prophesied under the same
four kings.[2]

While it may be a matter of curious speculation what
led to this particular arrangement of the Prophets,
it is of no especial moment, as it was neither ancient
nor authoritative. The passage in Baba Bathra, with
which we are now concerned, is preceded by inquiries,[3]

---

[1] Strack (p. 433) gives Geiger the credit of having established this
fact.

[2] So also Buhl, p. 38; Ryle, p. 228.

[3] Marx (p. 28) extracts the following from the tract Baba Bathra,
fol. 13b: "Our Rabbis taught, It is not forbidden to write the law,
prophets and hagiographa in one volume: these are the words of R.
Meir (an eminent doctor of the second century A.D., a pupil of R.
Akiba). R. Judah (either Ben-Hai, a contemporary of R. Meir, or
Ben-Bethera of the first century) says: The law ought to be written by
itself, the prophets by themselves, and the hagiographa by themselves.
Other scholars say: Each book should be written separately. R. Judah
defends his opinion by relating that Boethus ben-Zonin had the eight
prophets written together in one volume, and this was approved by
Eleazar ben-Azariah (President of the Synod along with the Patriarch
Gamaliel of the first century). But some say that the Prophets of Boethus were each written separately. The Rabbi (Judah ha-Kadosh,
writer of the Mishnah in the second century) said: They brought us the
law, prophets, and hagiographa combined in one volume, and we pronounced it all right."

"whether it is allowable to combine the law with the prophets and hagiographa in one volume; and in another place (Megillah, fol. 27a) the question is asked whether it is proper to lay books of the prophets on the volume of the law. These two questions show that at that time the Jews were not in the habit of writing all the sacred books in one volume. For, if they were, it would have been stated that they had very many books containing the entire Scriptures or all the prophets or all the hagiographa. Among these there certainly would have been several approved by distinguished Rabbis, and not merely a single volume of the prophets and one of the entire Old Testament of which mention is made. Synagogues also and schools would have been supplied with copies venerable from age, so that no one could have asked whether it was allowable to have copies of this sort. . . . We have tried in vain to discover a passage in the Talmud which speaks of a book of the prophets or a book of the hagiographa as a unit. Rabbis often mention old books which contained the whole law, but never books containing either all the prophets or all the hagiographa, except in that one passage of the tract Baba Bathra cited in the preceding note. . . . When now the question arose, what order should be adopted if all the sacred books were to be written in one volume, it is not surprising if some would think one order best and others another. We cannot consequently expect to find in the Talmud a legally required and anciently established order, but only what certain doctors thought true and right."[1]

It is evident from these considerations, as stated by Marx, that no more weight can be attributed to this order prescribed for the books of the prophets than to the speculations contained in the same para-

[1] Marx, pp. 29, 30, 33.

graph concerning the origin of the several books, see p. 94.

In the Talmudic order of the Hagiographa Ruth stands first. The question is asked why Job, whom they referred to the time of Moses, did not have the first place ; and the answer is given that it was not suitable to begin with calamity. The real reason for prefixing Ruth to the Psalms probably is that it records the ancestry of David, by whom so many of the Psalms were written. As some of the Psalms were attributed to Adam, Melchizedek and Abraham (though committed to writing by David), the Psalter is put before Job. Then follow the three books ascribed to Solomon, Proverbs, Ecclesiastes and Song of Songs ; then, in chronological order, the Lamentations of Jeremiah, Daniel, Esther, Ezra, and finally Chronicles, which was attributed to Ezra.

Another Baraitha[1] speaks of the Psalms, Proverbs, and Job as the three greater K'thubhim, and the Song of Songs, Ecclesiastes, and Lamentations as the lesser K'thubhim. Fürst (pp. 57, 60), without any reason, converts this into a distinction of older and more recent K'thubhim, and hence infers the gradual formation of this part of the canon ; that the Song of Songs and Ecclesiastes were a comparatively late addition, and that Esther had not yet been advanced to canonical dignity when this phraseology became current. But no such consequences follow from the use of this simple phrase. In the Talmudic arrangement the six poetical books stand together and spontaneously divide themselves into three of larger and three of smaller size.

The Talmudic arrangement of the books is only followed in a very limited number of Hebrew manuscripts, which are specified in detail by Strack (p. 441). The Massoretic arrangement, which according to Elias Levita

---

[1] Berachoth, fol. 57b.

is followed chiefly by the Spanish manuscripts, is in the Prophets: Isaiah, Jeremiah, Ezekiel, the Twelve; and in the Hagiographa: Chronicles, Psalms, Job, Proverbs, Ruth, Song of Songs, Ecclesiastes, Lamentations, Esther, Daniel, Ezra. In this order Isaiah is restored to its proper chronological place. Chronicles leads the Hagiographa because its genealogies begin with Adam; Ruth is transposed so as to stand with the smaller K'thubhim, and Esther is transposed with Daniel for a like reason.

The German manuscripts, followed by the printed editions of the Hebrew Bible, adopt a different order still in the Hagiographa. The three large poetical books stand first, Proverbs as the work of Solomon being transposed with Job, so as to stand next to the Psalms of David; then the five small books called Megilloth in the order of the festivals upon which they are read in the Synagogues; then Daniel, Ezra, and Nehemiah, chronologically disposed; and finally Chronicles, which with its genealogies and its history, extending from Adam to the end of the Babylonish exile, forms a suitable appendix to the entire volume of Scripture.

The Jewish authorities, whom Jerome followed in his Prologus Galeatus (his helmed prologue, intended as a defence against the intrusion of apocryphal books into the canon), joined Ruth with Judges, Lamentations with Jeremiah, and arranged the Hagiographa thus: Job, Psalms, Proverbs, Ecclesiastes, Song of Songs, Daniel, Chronicles, Ezra with Nehemiah, and Esther. Job is probably put before the Psalms on the assumption that it was written by Moses or in his time; Chronicles before Ezra as the proper historical order; and Esther last on the supposition shared by Josephus that Ezra and Nehemiah lived under Xerxes, and that Ahasuerus was his son Artaxerxes.

In the Septuagint the threefold division of the canon is abandoned, and the fourfold classification into the Law of Moses, the Historical, Poetical, and Prophetical Books substituted in its stead. It is not worth while here to detail the various arrangements of the books, which are found in early Christian catalogues and in the manuscripts of the Greek and Latin Bibles.[1]

There was a great diversity likewise in ancient catalogues in their enumeration of the books of the Old Testament, though without any real difference in the extent of the canon. The difference lay merely in the various modes of grouping and counting the very same books. We have already seen that it was usual to reckon Samuel, Kings, the twelve Minor Prophets and Chronicles as each one book, and to count Ezra and Nehemiah as together constituting one. Then (p. 87) if Ruth was joined to Judges, and Lamentations to Jeremiah, the total was 22; if Ruth and Lamentations were each counted separately, it was 24. The 22 books were sometimes divided into four Pentateuchs or groups of five : 1. The five books of Moses. 2. Five historical books, Joshua, Judges, Samuel, Kings, and Chronicles. 3. Five poetical books, Job, Psalms, Proverbs, Ecclesiastes, and Song of Solomon. 4. Five prophetical books, Isaiah, Jeremiah, Ezekiel, Daniel, and the Minor Prophets. Ezra and Esther were supernumeraries.

Epiphanius and Jerome mention that they were sometimes reckoned 27, or equal to the Hebrew alphabet with the five final letters added. Thus Jerome says : "As there are five letters with double forms in the alphabet, so there are five double books in the canon, viz. : Samuel, Kings, Chronicles, Ezra with Nehemiah, and Jeremiah

---

[1] Several of these are given in Ryle (pp. 213–218), and Excursus C (pp. 281, 282). And a much more detailed list may be found in Hody, De Bibliorum Textibus Originalibus (pp. 644–664).

with Lamentations." If each of the books thus paired together be counted separately, the whole number will be 27. Then if in addition Ruth be separated from Judges, the number will be 28.[1]

Again they have been counted 33, which, with the 27 books of the New Testament, makes 60 in the entire Bible, a number which was associated with the 60 queens of the Song of Solomon (vi. 8). This is made out by uniting the books as in counting 22, only reckoning the Minor Prophets as twelve instead of one. Finally, if all the books are counted separately, the number will be 39, as in the English Bible.

[1] So reckoned by John Ferus (A.D. 1540), as stated by Cosin, p. 202.

Twin Brooks Series

Barclay, William
  Educational Ideals in the Ancient World
Bass, Clarence B.
  Backgrounds to Dispensationalism
Battenhouse, Roy W. (ed.)
  A Companion to Study of St. Augustine
Bavinck, Herman
  The Doctrine of God
  Our Reasonable Faith
  The Philosophy of Revelation
Beardslee, John W., III (ed. & tr.)
  Reformed Dogmatics
Beckwith, Isbon T.
  The Apocalypse of John
Beecher, Willis Judson
  The Prophets and the Promise
Berkhof, Hendrikus
  Christ the Meaning of History
Berkhof, Louis
  The History of Christian Doctrines
  Introduction to Systematic Theology
Bright, John
  The Authority of the Old Testament
Bushnell, Horace
  Christian Nurture
Clark, Gordon H.
  Thales to Dewey
Dargan, Edwin C.
  History of Preaching
Davies, J. G.
  The Early Christian Church
Davis, John D.
  Genesis and Semitic Tradition
Deissmann, Adolf
  Light from the Ancient East
De Ridder, Richard R.
  Discipling the Nations
Eck, John
  Enchiridion of Commonplaces
Edersheim, Alfred
  The History of the Jewish Nation
  Prophecy and History
Farrar, Frederic W.
  History of Interpretation
Gerstner, John H.
  Reasons for Faith
  The Theology of the Major Sects
Goppelt, Leonhard
  Apostolic and Post-Apostolic Times
Green, William Henry
  General Introduction to the Old Testament
  The Higher Criticism of the Pentateuch
  The Unity of the Book of Genesis
Henry, Carl F. H.
  Aspects of Christian Social Ethics
  Christian Personal Ethics
Henry, Carl F. H. (ed.)
  Basic Christian Doctrines
  Fundamentals of the Faith
  Revelation and the Bible
Heppe, Heinrich
  Reformed Dogmatics
Hillerbrand, Hans J.
  The Reformation
Jerome
  Commentary on Daniel
Kevan, Ernest F.
  The Grace of Law
Klotsche, E. H.
  The History of Christian Doctrine

Kuiper, R. B.
  God-Centered Evangelism
Kurtz, J. H.
  Sacrificial Worship of the Old Testament
Kuyper, Abraham
  Principles of Sacred Theology
Law, Robert
  The Tests of Life
Lightfoot, J. B.
  The Apostolic Fathers
Longenecker, Richard N.
  Paul, Apostle of Liberty
Machen, J. Gresham
  The Virgin Birth of Christ
Manson, T. W.
  The Servant-Messiah
Mayor, Joseph B.
  The Epistle of James
  The Epistles of Jude and II Peter
McDonald, H. D.
  Theories of Revelation
Meeter, H. Henry
  The Basic Ideas of Calvinism
Orr, James
  Revelation and Inspiration
Rackham, Richard Belward
  The Acts of the Apostles
Ramm, Bernard
  Varieties of Christian Apologetics
Raven, John Howard
  The History of the Religion of Israel
Sandeen, Ernest R.
  The Roots of Fundamentalism
Seeberg, Reinhold
  Textbook of the History of Doctrines
Sherwin-White, A. N.
  Roman Society and Roman Law in the N. T.
Smith, David
  The Days of His Flesh
Smith, James
  The Voyage and Shipwreck of St. Paul
Stonehouse, Ned B.
  Origins of the Synoptic Gospels
  Witness of the Synoptic Gospels to Christ
Sweet, William Warren
  The Story of Religion in America
Theron, Daniel J.
  Evidence of Tradition
Trench, Richard Chenevix
  Notes on the Miracles of Our Lord
  Notes on the Parables of Our Lord
  Studies in the Gospels
Trueblood, David Elton
  General Philosophy
  Philosophy of Religion
Turretin, Francis
  The Atonement of Christ
Van Til, Henry
  The Calvinistic Concept of Culture
Vos, Geerhardus
  The Pauline Eschatology
Westcott, B. F.
  General Survey of History of Canon of N.T.
Wilson, Robert Dick
  Studies in the Book of Daniel
Young, Warren C.
  A Christian Approach to Philosophy

For a more detailed description of Baker Book House editions of theological classics, write:
Baker Book House, P. O. Box 6287, Grand Rapids, MI 49506.